D1212242

Women Music Makers

Also by Janet Nichols

American Music Makers

Women Music Makers

AN INTRODUCTION
TO WOMEN COMPOSERS

JANET NICHOLS

Walker and Company
New York

First published in the United States of America in 1992
by Walker Publishing Company, Inc.

Published simultaneously in Canada by Thomas Allen & Son
Canada, Limited, Markham, Ontario

Library of Congress Cataloging-in-Publication Data
Nichols, Janet, 1952–
Women music makers: an introduction to women composers / Janet
Nichols.
p.   cm.
Discography:
Includes bibliographical references and index.
Summary: Describes the lives and accomplishments of ten women
composers who challenged opposition because of their gender,
including Clara Schumann, Florence Price, and Ethel Smyth.
ISBN 0-8027-8168-3 (cloth). —ISBN 0-8027-8169-1
1. Women composers—Biography—Juvenile literature. [1. Women
composers.   2. Composers.]   I. Title.
ML3929.N5   1992
780'.92'2—dc20
[B]   91-47914
CIP
M AC

Printed in the United States of America
2   4   6   8   10   9   7   5   3   1

To my father,
William R. Nichols
And in memory of my mother,
Lena D. Nichols

CONTENTS

ACKNOWLEDGMENTS

I am most grateful to Laurie Anderson, Vivian Fine, Joan Tower, and Ellen Taaffe Zwilich for their cooperation and assistance in writing their respective chapters. All quotes and lyrics in the Laurie Anderson chapter are used with Laurie Anderson's permission and copyrighted by Difficult Music.

I wish to pay tribute to Nancy B. Reich for her brilliant book *Clara Schumann: The Artist and the Woman,* from which I drew much of my information on Schumann.

Thank you to Charlene M. Kaufmann, of the Department of Special Collections at the University of Arkansas, who photocopied and sent me stacks of information from the Florence Price Collection; and to the librarians at the Stanford University Music Library, University of California Music Library, and Visalia Public Library, who assisted me in locating research materials.

Thanks to my agent, Diana Finch, and to my editors, Bebe Willoughby and Amy Shields, for their continued encouragement and support in my writing books for young readers about music.

A special thank-you goes to my wonderful extended family, especially my mother-in-law, Jean Lynch; my sister-in-law, Kathleen Lynch; and my sister, Joyce Fanshier, who provided baby-sitting during my excursions to the Stanford and Cal music libraries. And to

Katie Lynch for all kinds of moral support; to my fun kids, Caitlin and Sean, who left me to write in peace every once in a while; and to my husband–best friend–patron–in-house consultant, Timothy Lynch, who makes my writing life what others can only dream about.

FOREWORD
HOW COME WE'VE NEVER HEARD OF THEM?

Bach, Beethoven, Chopin, Bartók—these are the composers I came to know while taking piano lessons as a young girl. I knew all of them were men, and I wondered why there were no women composers. The truth is that there are many women composers; I had just never heard of them! In writing this book, I discovered many reasons why most women composers aren't very well known.

For hundreds of years, music, like all the arts and sciences, was dominated by men who didn't believe that women were capable of doing notable work; therefore, these men didn't take women's efforts seriously. When music was published under a woman's name, music critics usually slashed it to pieces. For this reason, many women composers feared professional embarrassment and were hesitant to publish. Fanny Mendelssohn Hensel (1805–47) solved this problem by publishing her songs under her famous brother Felix's name.

A few men, however, did believe women were capable of composing. Robert Schumann encouraged his wife, Clara (1819–96), in her creative efforts, as did Clara's father, Friedrich Wieck. Clara, however, lacked confidence in herself and therefore produced relatively few compositions. She explained in her diary:

I once thought that I possessed creative talent, but I have given up this idea; a woman must not desire to compose—not one has

*been able to do it, and why should I expect to? It would be
arrogance.*

Clara's way of thinking was molded by the confines of
polite society, which for centuries believed that it was
"unladylike" and "inappropriate" for a woman to publish her works. When Barbara Strozzi (1619–64?) published her compositions, she was accused of being a
prostitute.

Yet some women ignored conventional thinking to
pursue a career in composition. Florence Price (1888–
1953), who suffered both sexual and racial prejudice,
knew that a black girl from Arkansas had little chance
of becoming a medical doctor, yet she refused to be
discouraged in the field of musical composition, which
offered even fewer opportunities for her.

Many women who were talented in composition
didn't have much time to pursue recognition because
their duty toward husband, children, and household
came first. Yet Fanny Mendelssohn Hensel solved that
problem by entertaining simply, paying very few social
calls, and throwing her energy into frequent musicales
that she presented in her own home. Clara Schumann,
the single parent of seven growing children, sent her
charges to boarding schools and commanded her large
brood by means of relentless correspondence with
housekeepers, governesses, teachers, and the children
themselves. (To seventeen-year-old Ferdinand's pro-
vider, Clara wrote, "At noon he should regularly have
as much meat as he wants, as he is growing frightfully
fast.") Both Florence Price and Vivian Fine (1913–)

raised families while juggling teaching and composing careers.

In the case of Amy Beach (1867–1944), her traditional role as a wife supported by a husband actually furthered her career as a composer. Amy bore no children and her husband's wealth and his old-fashioned insistence that she not work (as a concert pianist) allowed her many hours to pursue composition. In fact, Amy Beach is one of the few composers—men or women—who *never* had to worry about money. Perhaps that is why she honored her husband by signing her compositions "Mrs. H.H.A. Beach." It is interesting to note further that of the ten women composers in this book, six did not have children.

In 1928, novelist Virginia Woolf wrote these famous words: "A woman must have money and a room of her own if she is to write fiction." To write music, a woman must have much more than that, as Virginia's friend Dame Ethel Smyth (1858–1944) very well knew. In order to get a major orchestral work or opera performed, a composer needs money, support, connections, name recognition, self-confidence, and a good amount of gumption. Ethel Smyth was one of the few women who possessed all of these. She traipsed through all of Europe, arranged appointments with major musical directors, and sang and played on the piano her entire operas in hopes of getting them produced. In order to have her Mass in D performed, Ethel got Empress Eugénie of France to finance it, then asked her friend Lady Ponsonby to ask her husband, Sir Henry, to speak to the Duke of Edinburgh, who engaged conductor Sir Joseph Barnby and the Royal Choral Society for the occasion.

On-the-job training is essential in all occupations, and composing is no exception. Yet most positions in music were closed to women. For centuries, women instrumentalists and singers were banned in most churches and theaters. As late as 1940, women players were excluded from most major orchestras. For this reason, women composers tended not to write large works for orchestra and opera, which might receive wide acclaim and notoriety, but instead composed smaller pieces for fewer players and singers, to be performed in the home. As positions in orchestras opened up to women, women became more able to compose for them. In the sixties Ellen Taaffe Zwilich (1939–   ) spent part of her apprenticeship playing violin in the American Symphony Orchestra.

At last, as we near the twenty-first century, women composers are gaining their just recognition. Their works are being more widely published, performed, and recorded. Names such as those of Pulitzer Prize winners Ellen Taaffe Zwilich and Shulamit Ran, Grawemeyer Award winner Joan Tower, and performance artist Laurie Anderson are beginning to sound familiar.

Throughout the ages, women composers' struggle to be heard has been hard and relentless. Here, in *Women Music Makers*, a small part of that drama unfolds.

Women Music Makers

Barbara Strozzi is probably the woman in this painting, "Female Musician with Viola da Gamba" by Bernardo Strozzi (no relation to Barbara)
Dresden, Staatliche Kunstsammlungen

One
BARBARA STROZZI
(1619–64?)

◆

Barbara Strozzi lived during the Baroque era, which spans the long time in music history between 1600 and 1750. During the Baroque era, a musician was a tradesman, just like a baker, tailor, or carpenter. A boy usually learned his trade from his father, who had learned it from *his* father. Generation after generation, the members of one family shared the same occupation. Boys from poor families who knew no trade sometimes went to live with tradesmen to learn a way to make a living.

Musicians were employed by churches, royal courts, towns, and theaters. They were expected to compose and perform new music for each special occasion or concert. Musicians composed to meet the needs of their positions. For instance, when Johann Sebastian Bach worked for the prince of Cöthen he entertained the prince by composing his beautiful *Brandenburg Concertos* for the court orchestra to play. Later, when Bach was the director of music of St. Thomas Church in Leipzig, he composed music for church services, including his famous Mass in B Minor. Bach would be very surprised to know that his music is still being performed today. He composed it only for the occasion for which it was needed. He was only doing his job.

But most jobs in music weren't open to women. Women were not allowed to hold positions as singers or instrumentalists in the Church. A few women were opera singers, although the pope, the head of the Church, banned them from appearing onstage in Rome and other parts of Italy. We know of only three women who received payment for playing musical instruments in Italian theaters from 1550 to 1700. Women certainly didn't hold positions as music directors, conductors, or heads of opera companies. Therefore, women received no on-the-job training, and they had no incentive to compose to meet the needs of a professional position.

And yet, between 1566 and 1700, no fewer than twenty-three Italian women composed works of such high caliber that their work was accepted for publication. Many other women composed, but either they performed their works without notating them, or their handwritten manuscripts no longer survive. Most of these women were able to work in music only because they lived in royal courts or in convents.

Throughout Europe, the ruling class lived in hundreds of royal courts. They spent their great wealth on magnificent palaces and lavish entertainment. Each court hired its own private music director, orchestra, and singers—who at first were all men. Around 1580, members of the Italian court of Ferrara began to appreciate that female singers had a high silvery tone that men could not duplicate. The Ferrara court hired an ensemble of the finest women singers and paid them high wages to perform daily concerts. Other courts caught on to the idea, and soon professional women singers were in great demand. For the first time, it became highly profitable for tradesmen to give their daughters musical training in hopes that they would be accepted as court singers. Because of their musical education, these women singers were able to compose vocal music for their own performances.

One court singer-composer was Francesca Caccini, born in 1587. Her father, the famous composer Giulio Caccini, taught her singing and composition at a very young age. She became the highest-paid singer in the Florentine court. At one time, only the duke's secretary drew a salary larger than hers. Francesca Caccini composed musical settings for whole plays that were written by famous dramatists. The quality of her compositions equals that of music by any male composer of her time.

Other women composers lived in convents. Of the twenty-three published women composers mentioned earlier, most were nuns. Nuns enjoyed much more artistic freedom than did women who lived outside convent walls, in the society of men. At the end of the sixteenth century, the convents in Milan became especially famous for their outstanding work in music. People traveled long distances to hear the nuns sing and play string, wind, and keyboard instruments at their church services.

The nun Isabella Leonarda of Novara composed an amazing number of works. By 1700, the year she turned eighty, Leonarda had produced twenty books of music, mostly religious songs for solo voice and choir. She also was the first woman to publish trio sonatas (music written for two violins and keyboard).

In the mid-1500s, the pope decided that everyone was having too much fun making beautiful music in church and not thinking enough about God. In 1545, he called a meeting, the Council of Trent, in which he put harsh restrictions on church music. Nuns were commanded to return to the ancient sacred music known as Gregorian chant, and could perform new, elaborate music only on special occasions. The only instrument they could play was the organ. Musicians couldn't come into the convent to teach music to the nuns, nor could the nuns leave the convent to study elsewhere. Isabella Leonarda and the other composer-nuns must have disobeyed these rules to produce their works. As time went on, the laws were more strictly enforced. By 1700, the era of nun as composer came to an end.

A position as a court singer was very hard to obtain, and a woman could work in music in a convent only if she wanted to become a nun. Barbara Strozzi was neither a court singer nor a nun. Giulio Strozzi, her adoptive father, offered her a unique situation that gave her an opportunity to develop as a composer. Since women composers were not allowed *out* in society, Giulio brought society *into* his own home, so that his daughter could be a part of it.

Not much is known about Barbara's life. She was born in Venice in 1619. Her mother was Isabella Garzoni, an unmarried servant of the writer Giulio Strozzi. Her biological father is unknown, although he may very well have been Giulio.

Giulio Strozzi was a well-known poet and dramatist. His friends were the important writers, painters, and musicians of Venice. The early 1600s were an exciting time to be an artist in Venice. Opera had just been born, and from the beginning it was a spectacular and popular entertainment. Venice soon became the opera center of the world. The first important opera composer, Claudio Monteverdi, lived and produced operas in Venice, and so did his pupil Francesco Cavalli. Giulio Strozzi wrote librettos—plays for operas—which both Monteverdi and Cavalli set to music. As one of the first librettists, Giulio helped develop opera from its earliest stages.

When Barbara was nine, Giulio included her in his will, referring to her as Barbara Valle. In his last will, signed twenty-two years later, he made her his sole heir and called her Barbara Strozzi. At some time, he must have adopted Barbara legally. He treated her like his own daughter from a very early age. He recognized her musical talent and did much to help her in a career as a professional musician, even though proper Venetian women didn't have careers. When Barbara was about ten, Giulio arranged for her to take singing and composition lessons from Cavalli. Barbara's study with Cavalli lasted about seven years.

By the age of sixteen, Barbara was performing in her father's home for his important guests. When she sang, she probably accompanied herself with a lute, a small stringed instrument with a pear-shaped body, similar to a guitar. A published article described her singing style as bold and graceful.

In 1637, Giulio started an academy in his home, called Accademia degli Unisoni. Giulio's "academy" was not really a school as we know it, but more like a private club for learned men. Its membership included all the important poets, dramatists, writers, philosophers, and historians in Venice. The men attended meetings to discuss the social issues of their time. Ironically, though women were not allowed membership in the academy, Barbara acted as its hostess and mascot. At the meetings, she took part in the men's discussions and sang, accompanying herself on the lute. In fact, it seems that the main reason Giulio established the academy was so all the right people in Venice could hear Barbara sing her compositions.

The academy issued publications that were dedicated to Barbara. One publication of 1638 listed the members' names and described the activities in three of their meetings. At all three meetings, the men discussed the subject of love and Barbara sang. She was also the judge of one debate, and awarded prizes to the best speakers. At one meeting, Barbara read aloud an argument on the question, Which is the better weapon in love—tears or song? At the end of the reading, she gave her own opinion on the subject. She thought song was more powerful than tears. The men wouldn't have come to the meeting, she reasoned, "[if] I invited you to see me cry rather than to hear me sing."

Feminism was another subject of interest for the members of the academy. They held views about women that were liberal for their time. Unlike the author of a series of newly published pamphlets, the academy members believed that women had souls and that they were indeed members of the human race! These wise men also respected Barbara's compositions, even though a woman had written them.

In 1644, at the age of twenty-five, Barbara Strozzi had her first book of music published. It was a collection of madrigals—songs set for two to five voices— with texts written by Giulio. Barbara knew she was making a daring move. In the dedication of her book to the grand duchess of Tuscany, Barbara wrote: "As a woman I publish all too boldly." She also expected to receive "thunderbolts of slander."

The "thunderbolts" struck hard indeed. An anonymous writer published a series of articles poking fun at Barbara and the academy. The writer suggested that her music making and her keeping company with so many men meant that she was a prostitute. He even tried to explain why she never became pregnant!

In 1651, Strozzi published her second book of songs, which she dedicated to Ferdinand II of Austria to celebrate his marriage to Eleanor of Mantua. Giulio died the following March, leaving Barbara a very small inheritance. In fact, he didn't even have enough money to cover the cost of his own funeral.

Barbara worked very hard after her father's death, writing enough vocal music to fill one volume each year for the next five years. She dedicated her published works to royalty and wealthy people, in hopes of getting a steady patron or a position as a court composer. She was never successful at either. However, through her published works, her fame and popularity grew. In the dedication of her fifth book, she mentioned that her "feminine weaknesses" didn't limit her capabilities as a composer. In her last three dedications, she didn't mention her sex at all. Apparently, she had become so successful that the fact that she was a woman no longer mattered. Her works appeared in other publications besides her own, along with those of the most important composers of her time, including her teacher, Francesco Cavalli.

Strozzi's songs are almost all about unhappiness in love, just like many pop songs recorded today. Strozzi's songs, however, aren't slow and sad. The tempo is often lively, and the character singing the song has a strong spirit, no matter how much her lover has wronged her.

Three of Strozzi's longest works are cantatas, which tell stories. A cantata, which is a piece to sing, is quite long, with several different sections. One of Strozzi's is actually a news item of 1642, about Henri de Cinq-

Mars, a member of the court of King Louis XIII of France. Cinq-Mars plotted against the statesman Richelieu, and the king condemned him to death. At the end of this dramatic song, Cinq-Mar's head is cut off, and, at the same moment, stormy waves rise up on the River Seine.

Strozzi shows much imagination in making the drama of words come alive in her music. She often uses word painting, which reflects the meaning of a word in a musical idea. In the following short excerpt from "Gite, o giorni dolenti" ("Pass, O Sorrowful Days"), Strozzi uses word painting three times.

> *Among the trumpets of Mars*
> *And the clamorous noise of war,*
> *The merry god of wedding descends to earth . . .*

On the word "trumpet," Strozzi has the singer sing a skipping melody similar to a trumpet call. The first part is sung loud and the second part is sung very soft, in imitation of how a trumpet sound would echo. At "clamorous noise of war," the voice and accompaniment are loud and agitated. At "descends to earth," the singer starts at the very top of her range and sings down two octaves to the very bottom of her range.

Strozzi also uses many contrasts in her music. She starts with a slow tempo, then speeds up to a fast tempo. A very loud phrase is followed by a very soft one. She changes the meter from duple (an accent every two beats) to triple (an accent every three beats).

Sometimes she starts with the high range of the voice, then suddenly jumps to the low range.

Strozzi increases excitement by repeating an important word or phrase. In one of her songs she clamors, "Betrayal! Betrayal! Betrayal!" which is certainly more powerful than using the word only once.

For a single, vivid word like "flames" or "trembling," Strozzi gives the singer many, many notes to sing. For a long, lofty moment, the voice breaks free of words, and runs, leaps, and soars all on its own, just like other musical instruments.

Barbara Strozzi's eighth and last volume of songs was published in 1664, and then she disappeared from history. No one knows what happened to her, nor how, when, and where she died.

During Barbara Strozzi's lifetime, many articles were published about her beautiful singing voice. The difficulty of her own compositions shows what an accomplished singer she must have been.

At that time in Venice, most singers became famous by singing opera. Barbara's teacher was an opera composer, and her father was a librettist. Yet Barbara composed no operas. There is no record of her ever singing in an opera or in any public concert hall.

Apparently, Barbara Strozzi never performed anywhere but in her own home. She became an expert in writing chamber vocal works, music meant to be sung in a small room rather than a large opera house or concert hall. She composed over a hundred songs, including many for solo voice with keyboard or lute accompaniment. The large number and the high quality of her compositions make her one of the most important composers of chamber vocal music of the Baroque era. She may be the only composer in all of history who earned wide acclaim without ever leaving her own home.

This sketch of Fanny Mendelssohn Hensel was drawn by her husband, Wilhelm Hensel
The Mendelssohn Family, *Sebastian Hensel (New York: Harper and Brothers, 1882)*

TWO
FANNY MENDELSSOHN HENSEL
(1805–47)

A girl named Fanny and a boy named Felix were born into the Mendelssohn family, one of the most intelligent and gifted families of the early nineteenth century. Fanny, born on November 14, 1805, and Felix, born February 3, 1809, inherited great musical talent from their mother, Leah. Both children were given nearly the same, thorough musical education. However, as Fanny neared her fifteenth birthday, her father, Abraham, wrote her a letter indicating that his expectations for her were far different than those he had for Felix:

Music will perhaps become [Felix's] profession, whilst for you it can and must only be an ornament, never the root of your being

13

*and doing. . . . Your very joy at the praise he earns proves that
you might, in his place, have merited equal approval. Remain
true to these sentiments and to this line of conduct; they are
feminine, and only what is truly feminine is an ornament to
your sex.*

The dutiful daughter took this advice to heart. Although Fanny Mendelssohn Hensel wrote over four
hundred compositions, only a few have been published.
While every music-history book about the Romantic
era is filled with praise for the Mendelssohn boy, the
Mendelssohn girl is rarely mentioned on a single page;
it is as if she never existed. Certainly her life and works
deserve a closer look.

Besides Fanny and Felix, there were two other Mendelssohn children: Rebecca, born April 11, 1911, and
Paul, born October 30, 1913. Their grandfather was
the famous Jewish philosopher Moses Mendelssohn. In
Moses' time, Jewish people lived in ghettos, spoke only
Yiddish, and were denied most civil rights. The Jewish
religion did not allow Jews to read anything about their
Christian neighbors, nor did the Christians allow the
Jews access to their books. Moses felt that this igno-
rance on both sides was the reason his people had been
downtrodden for so many years. He read forbidden
books in secret, and taught himself German as well as
many other languages. He wrote many books, but most
important, he translated the Yiddish Bible into German so that other Jews could learn the language.
Although Moses never had very much money, he was
rich in the company he kept. His house was open to

the most brilliant men of his time, both Jewish and Christian.

Moses had a humpback and a stammer, but he also had a good sense of humor and was very wise. Fromet Gugenheim, the girl he was to marry, admired his writings but was quite shocked when she first met him and saw his humpback. Moses noticed her distaste and told her this story:

> When a Jewish child is born, proclamation is made in heaven of the name of the person that he or she will some day marry. When I was born, my future wife was also named, but at the same time it was said that she herself would be humpbacked. "O God," I said, "a deformed girl will lead an unhappy life. Dear Lord, give the humpback to me, and let the girl be flawless and beautiful."

After hearing this story, Fromet was very happy to become Moses' wife.

The law decreed that every Jewish couple about to be married had to buy china from the royal china factory. The newlyweds were not allowed to choose their purchases, but were instead forced to buy whatever the factory manager wanted to get rid of. Apparently, oversized porcelain apes weren't selling well the year Moses and Fromet were to be married. The engaged couple got stuck with *twenty* of the breakable beasts. The ape figurines were passed down from generation to generation as a family joke and an ironic symbol of Jewish oppression.

The king of Prussia, Frederick the Great, despised Jews, but he had also heard of Moses' wisdom. One day, supposedly, he called the philosopher to his palace to help him make an important decision of state. When Moses arrived at the gate, stooped and poorly dressed, the guard would not let him in until he stated why he had come. "I am a juggler," said Moses. Later, the king asked Moses why he had lied. Moses replied, "Because I know it is easier for a juggler to get into your palace than a philosopher."

Fanny would inherit her grandfather's delightful blend of wit and wisdom, as well as a small curve of the spine, which slightly raised one of her shoulders.

When Moses died at age fifty-seven, he left his wife and six children in poverty. However, his oldest son, Joseph, and Fanny and Felix's father, Abraham, co-founded a bank, Mendelssohn and Company, in Hamburg, and became quite wealthy. Abraham married Leah Salomon, a rich and highly educated Jewish woman who could speak four languages and was an accomplished amateur pianist. Leah read Greek in secret because women who were very intelligent were not considered feminine.

Leah was her children's first piano teacher. She began teaching each child when he or she was four years old, starting with instruction periods of five minutes, then lengthening them as the child got older. For many years, Fanny and Felix practiced their lessons only when their mother could sit nearby, knitting and calling out corrections.

Both Fanny and Felix inherited their grandfather's great desire for knowledge. Abraham spared no expense in hiring the very best teachers for his children.

The family lived in Paris in 1816 so that Fanny and Felix could study piano with the renowned concert artist Mademoiselle Marie Bigot. Four years later, Fanny and Felix studied piano with Ludwig Berger and composition with Carl Friedrich Zelter in Berlin, where the Mendelssohns made their permanent home in 1811.

When Fanny was thirteen, she surprised her father on his birthday by performing—from memory—the twenty-four preludes from Johann Sebastian Bach's *Well-Tempered Clavier*, a collection of difficult piano pieces. On Abraham's next birthday, Fanny composed for him her first song.

The Mendelssohn children liked to stage theatrical productions to entertain their parents and family friends. Fanny and Felix put on a series of Shakespearean plays in which they assigned parts to Rebecca and Paul. Their favorite play was *A Midsummer Night's Dream*; they took turns playing all the parts. The children also "published" a newspaper. In summer it was called *The Garden Times* and in winter *The Tea and Snow Times*. Actually, the newspaper was more like an open journal, with pens and an inkwell nearby. Everyone who passed through the Mendelssohn home was expected to contribute and, at the end of each day, the "newspaper" was read aloud.

The Mendelssohn family continued the tradition Moses had begun by opening their home to the most learned men of their time. Fanny and Felix had the opportunity to meet and talk with the renowned poets Goethe, Heinrich Heine, and Joseph von Eichendorff, writer Jean Paul, scientist Alexander von Humboldt, philosopher Georg Wilhelm Friedrich Hegel, and actor Eduard Devrient.

The Mendelssohns, however, did not follow the traditions of the Jewish religion. Grandfather Moses didn't realize that when he broke down the barriers between the Jewish and Christian worlds, he also did away with many of the differences. Many Jewish people converted to Christianity in hopes of being accepted into European society. Moses would have been shocked to know that his own grandchildren were baptized and confirmed in the Lutheran church of Germany. Abraham wanted to raise his children as Jews, but Leah's wealthy and childless brother, Jakob Bartholdy, badgered him into having the children converted. Bartholdy's original name was Salomon, like Leah's maiden name, but he changed it to a more Christian-sounding name when he became a Christian himself. Uncle Jakob argued that prejudice against Jews would prevent his nephews from succeeding in their chosen careers. He also convinced Abraham to add "Bartholdy" to their name to preserve his "memory in the family"; he reasoned that in other countries a man often added the name of his wife's family onto his own. Abraham and Leah had difficulty being the Jewish parents of Christian children, so they converted to Christianity six years after their children.

The Mendelssohn children did not accept these changes in name and religion without question. Over and over, Abraham had to explain the changes to them. When he had calling cards printed up for his son reading: "Felix M. Bartholdy," Felix refused to use them. On concert programs his name always appeared as "Felix Mendelssohn." For a while, Rebecca signed her name "Rebecca *meden* Bartholdy," *"meden"* being Greek for "never." Fanny and Rebecca eventually solved the name problem by taking their husbands' names after marriage.

Fanny met her future husband in January 1821, when Nicholas, heir to the throne of Russia, came to Berlin to visit the court of the king of Prussia, Frederick William III. The two royal families staged a magnificent drama for the awestruck common people. A painter, Wilhelm Hensel, was called in to paint the portraits of the royal actors dressed in the authentic Oriental costumes they wore in the play. Wilhelm put his paintings on exhibit at his studio and the Mendelssohn family went to see them.

Wilhelm looked at Fanny; Fanny looked at Wilhelm; and, supposedly, they fell in love on the spot. Wilhelm, twenty-eight, began to court seventeen-year-old Fanny. Abraham and Leah did not approve of Wilhelm as a suitor for their daughter. They allowed him to visit her in their home but received him coolly.

Wilhelm Hensel was the son of a poor country clergyman, beneath Fanny's station in life. He had come to Berlin nearly penniless and had taught himself painting. Abraham and Leah doubted that he could comfortably support a wife. Leah secretly suspected that Wilhelm was a gold-digger, hoping to marry a girl from a wealthy family to support his art.

But Wilhelm was very talented and ambitious. He

won a Prussian government scholarship to study classical art in Rome for several years. He was delighted with
the opportunity, but he worried that another man
would steal Fanny's affections during his absence. He
asked Abraham and Leah if he and Fanny could become formally engaged before his departure. The Mendelssohns turned him down flat.

Leah even forbade Wilhelm to write to Fanny while
he was in Rome. This seems especially cruel, but Leah
was a wise woman who knew what was best for her
daughter. She didn't want Fanny mooning around for
a boyfriend who would be absent for several long years.
Leah wrote Wilhelm:

> *You must not be angry with me. . . . Fanny is very young. . . .*
> *I will not have you, by love-letters, transport her for years into*
> *a state of consuming passion and a yearning frame of mind quite*
> *strange to her character, when I have her now before me*
> *blooming, healthy, happy, and free.*

Wilhelm understood Leah's reasoning and vowed to
respect her wishes. He drew sketches of all the Mendelssohn family members to remember them by while
he was away. In Rome, Wilhelm met Jakob Bartholdy,
who was an avid patron of the arts. Uncle Jakob was
impressed with Wilhelm's talents and commissioned
him to paint a fresco that covered an entire wall of his
home. Through Jakob's letters, Leah was able to get a
different view of Wilhelm, which was probably quite
favorable.

Wilhelm, however, found his own way into Leah's

heart. He made many drawings of the Mendelssohn family, each of them with Fanny as the central character, then sent them one by one with a letter to Leah. Wilhelm's love for Fanny shone through his art, and soon Leah began reading his letters aloud to Fanny.

Wilhelm was in Rome so long that his sketches became outdated. In thanking him for a drawing, Leah wrote:

> I cannot tell you how much its exquisite beauty of execution and fine delicate idea has surprised and touched us. The spiritualised, à la Hensel idealized likeness of the four children has not escaped our eyes. Although since your absence they have so much changed and grown, and somehow got coarse-grained, that your ideal likeness only represents them as they were. . . .

While Wilhelm pursued his work in Rome, Fanny wasted no time in sitting idle and waiting for her sweetheart to come home. She continued to spend much of her time practicing the piano and composing. In 1822, the Mendelssohn family began staging musicales in their home, every other Sunday morning. Their residence, 3 Leipzigerstrasse, soon became one of the most fashionable salons in Europe. While Abraham and Leah didn't consider it proper for their daughter to perform in public, they encouraged Fanny to perform at the family's musicales. She and Felix played the piano, Rebecca sang, and Paul played the cello. The Mendelssohns hired a small orchestra and chorus to perform Felix's compositions, which he conducted.

Clearly Felix was the star of these musicales; how-

This Victorian artist's conception of the Mendelssohns' family musicales shows Felix, age thirteen, conducting in the limelight, while Fanny, age seventeen, sits in his shadow
The Great Composers, J. Stieler (London, 1879)

ever, he was fiercely proud of Fanny's accomplishments in music. Often when people praised him for his piano playing, Felix remarked, "But you should hear my sister Fanny!" In fact, between sister and brother, there was a near-telepathic bond, the kind that is often found in identical twins. Fanny's and Felix's compositional styles are quite similar. They both use strict classical forms of the previous era, combined with adventurous harmonies in the Romantic spirit.

Felix and Fanny took turns playing and critiquing each other's works. Fanny had an annoying habit of making little coughing sounds when she didn't like something Felix had composed; he made them both laugh by imitating her. Felix showed Fanny everything he composed, so that when she was seventeen and he was thirteen, she proudly wrote in her diary:

> *I have watched his progress step by step, and may say I have contributed to his development. I have always been his only musical advisor and he never writes down a thought before submitting it to my judgment. I have known his operas by heart before a note was written.*

In 1827, at the age of twenty-two, Fanny had developed into a mature composer, so that her music was ready for publication. However, Abraham and Leah did not think it was appropriate or ladylike for her to publish her work. The compositions of women who dared to publish were never taken seriously, but were instead cast off as merely "women's work." Women's compositions were often severely criticized in published reviews. To protect Fanny from such embarrassment, Felix published her music under his name. Three of her songs—"The Home Spell," "Italy," and "Suleika and Hatem"—appeared in his collection of *Lieder* (German for "songs"), Opus 8. Several years later, another three songs—"Sleepless," "Forsaken," and "The Nun"—were included in his *Lieder*, Opus 9.

Fanny Mendelssohn Hensel's songs are considered some of the finest written during the Romantic era. In most of them the piano plays a duet with the voice, rather than merely supporting it. Sometimes the rhythm and melody of the voice are quite simple so the words can be easily understood, while the piano accompaniment is more intricate. Hensel's phrase lengths are varied to create interest, flow, and expression. The texts of Hensel's songs are almost always poems written by famous German poets who lived during her lifetime. Goethe, Heinrich Heine, and Joseph von Eichendorff.

By 1828, Wilhelm Hensel had spent five long years in Rome, apart from Fanny. Jakob Bartholdy died, and, as expected, Leah inherited his fortune. Wilhelm was appointed executor of Jakob's vast art collection and it took him quite a long time to sell or distribute it to other collectors and museums.

Finally, in October, Wilhelm returned to Berlin. He hardly recognized his Fanny, who was now twenty-three and no longer considered young. Family friends had begun to joke that Fanny would marry Felix, a joke Leah didn't appreciate. Even so, Abraham and Leah were not happy that Wilhelm was again asking for Fanny's hand in marriage. But, for once, Fanny rebelled against her parents' wishes: She insisted on marrying Wilhelm. Abraham and Leah had no choice but to accept him into the family graciously. Wilhelm and Fanny's engagement was announced on January 22, 1829, with the wedding date set for October 3.

Fanny was very happy about her upcoming marriage, but she also worried that it would draw her further apart from Felix, who by then was one of the most successful composers in Europe and often away from home. She became even more upset when news came from London that he had badly injured his knee in a carriage accident and would therefore miss her wedding. Felix consoled Fanny by writing: "Whether I address my sister henceforth as Mademoiselle or Madame means little. What is there in a name!"

The wedding took place in a modest Lutheran church. Fanny composed her own wedding music, which was played on the organ. After the ceremony, Fanny and Wilhelm took up residence in a small house that stood in the seven-acre garden behind 3 Leipzigerstrasse. Their only child, a son named Sebastian, was born the following June. He would become the author of a two-volume history, *The Mendelssohn Family*, based on numerous excerpts from journals and letters.

A few years after Sebastian's birth, Rebecca married mathematician Gustav Dirichlet and left home. The Hensels moved into the big roomy house with Abraham, Leah, and Paul. Fanny kept very busy raising Sebastian, housekeeping, and practicing the piano and composing. However, she was sometimes depressed about not having anyone with whom to share musical

ideas. She felt so isolated in her composing that she
became discouraged with her work. On July 15, 1836,
she wrote to a friend:

> Once a year, perhaps, some one will copy a piece of mine, or
> ask me to play something special—certainly not oftener; and
> now that Rebecca has left off singing, my songs lie unheeded
> and unknown. If nobody ever offers an opinion or takes the
> slightest interest in one's production, one loses . . . not only all
> pleasure in them, but all power of judging their value. Felix . . .
> is so seldom here that he cannot help me much, and thus I am
> thrown back on myself. But my own delight in music and
> Hensel's sympathy keep me awake still, and I cannot help
> considering it a sign of talent that I do not give it up, though I
> can get nobody to take an interest in my efforts.

Wilhelm saw how unhappy Fanny was and urged her
to publish her work. Leah also began to think that her
daughter's compositions deserved more recognition and
wrote to Felix, asking him to encourage her to publish.
Felix, however, still believed that it was not proper. He
wrote his mother:

> This is contrary to my views and to my convictions. . . .
> [Fanny] has neither inclination nor vocation for authorship. She
> is too much all that a woman ought to be for this. She regulates
> her house, and neither thinks of the public nor of the musical
> world, nor even of music at all, until her first duties are fulfilled.
> Publishing would only disturb her in these, and I cannot say
> that I approve of it.

For once, Felix was mistaken about his sister. Fanny
thought only about music. She had no interest in

expensive dresses, lavish dinner parties, or other luxu-
ries. She despised making calls and being called upon,
and she avoided social duties as much as possible.
Fanny felt very disappointed and discouraged by Felix's
opinion. She allowed only a single song to be included
in a collection of other composers' works, then wrote
Felix:

> In regard to my [plans to] publish, . . . Hensel is for it, you are
> against it. In any other matter I'd naturally accede entirely to
> the wishes of my husband, but in this matter alone it's crucial
> to have your approval.

Felix, of course, also did not approve of Fanny
performing in public. At the age of thirty-three she
gave the only public performance of her life. On
February 27, 1838, she played Felix's Piano Concerto
No. 1 in G Minor, Opus 25, for a charity benefit in a
Berlin concert hall. Fanny played down the importance
of the concert by calling it "one of those amateur
affairs where the tickets are twice the usual price, and
the chorus is composed of countesses, ambassadresses,
and officers."

In 1839 and 1840, the Hensel family toured Italy,
visiting Milan, Venice, and Florence, then settling for
several months in Rome. This was one of the happiest
times of Fanny's life. She met many musicians and had
many opportunities to perform in their homes. Her
inspiration was renewed and she composed many
pieces.

In 1842, seven years after Abraham's death, Leah

also died. Fanny took over managing the huge house at 3 Leipzigerstrasse and hostessing the family's Sunday morning musicales. Fanny did not entertain in Leah's lavish fashion, but instead kept arrangements as simple as possible. She threw her energy into composing, practicing, and rehearsing the chorus for the musicales.

In 1846, two rival Berlin publishing houses competed in bidding on Fanny's compositions. Fanny could not refuse the generous offers, despite Felix's feelings about her publishing. She choose a small number of what she thought were her best works and published two books of songs, a collection of piano pieces, and a book of choral works. The publication earned Fanny modest acclaim, which encouraged her to compose a larger work, her successful Piano Trio in D Minor, Opus 11, for violin, cello, and piano.

At forty-two, Fanny felt that her career as a composer had finally been launched. She had written every type of composition except an opera, including the Overture in C Major for orchestra; a piano trio; a piano quartet; a string quartet; a cello sonata; organ solos; and numerous songs and piano pieces. In May 1847, she wrote in her diary:

> *When in the morning after breakfasting with Wilhelm we each go to our own work, with a pleasant day to look back upon and another to look forward to. I am quite overcome with my own happiness.*

This was one of the last entries Fanny Mendelssohn Hensel made in her diary. On Friday, May 14, 1847, while she was rehearsing her chorus for the Sunday musicale, her hands slippped from the piano keys and fell useless to her sides. She could not move or speak. Soon she slipped into unconsciousness.

Sixteen-year-old Sebastian was called from his drawing lesson to fetch the doctor. He recalled that "I ran with all my might, and know that I kept saying to myself the whole while: 'It can't be anything serious, nothing bad can happen to us. . . .' "

But it was serious. Fanny had suffered a massive stroke: A major blood vessel had burst in her brain. She died at eleven o'clock in the evening. That Sunday, the piano in the grand hall of 3 Leipzigerstrasse was replaced with Fanny's coffin. Wilhelm sketched a likeness of his deceased wife, the hardest thing he ever had to do.

When Felix received the news of Fanny's death, he cried out and collapsed to the floor unconscious. The shock may have caused him to suffer a minor stroke. So close were sister and brother, that when Fanny died, perhaps a part of Felix died, too. He was too ill to travel to Berlin to attend the funeral.

Felix's wife, Cécile, whisked him off to Switzerland and then to the German resort of Baden-Baden. Nothing cured him of his grief and insomnia. He visited 3 Leipzigerstrasse and found the house and garden exactly as Fanny had left them. The realization of his bitter loss caused him to suffer another breakdown. By then, Wilhelm was nearly insane with grief. Although he had enough commissions to keep him busy for many years, he could no longer paint; nor could he care for his son. Sebastian was adopted into his aunt Rebecca's household. (Wilhelm lived aimlessly for fifteen more years, until he died of injuries he incurred while saving a child from being run over by a carriage.)

When Felix returned to Leipzig, he could no longer conduct or teach, and he composed very little. On a walk with Cécile on October 28, 1847, he could not raise his feet, but merely shuffled. He collapsed on their doorstep with a stroke. On November 3, he had another stroke. The following day, only six months after Fanny's death, Felix, aged thirty-eight, was also dead.

In 1858, Rebecca died suddenly of a massive stroke at age forty-seven. Moses, Abraham, Leah, and many of the Mendelssohn children's aunts, uncles, and cousins died of strokes. The Mendelssohns suffered from a genetic defect that produced weak blood vessels in the brain.

Stress may have brought on Fanny's stroke so early in her life. She suffered from constant inner turmoil resulting from conflicting goals. She had a strong creative urge to compose and perform, yet she felt compelled to attend to her household responsibilities first. She was born with phenomenal musical talent, and her parents had given her the best training to develop it; yet when it came time to show what she could do, her family denied her access to the professional world. Fanny's greatest source of inspiration and encouragement was her brother Felix; but he, too, discouraged her from making the most of her career.

Nevertheless, she dauntlessly worked within the confines of her circumstances, doing the best she could.

Without publishing, traveling extensively, performing in public, and interacting with other musicians, Fanny Mendelssohn Hensel never had much response to her music, and therefore never completely developed her talents. Even so, to set history straight: There were *two* formidable composers born to the Mendelssohn family. One was a man; one was a *woman.*

Clara Schumann, age thirty-eight. Photo by Hanfstaengl, 1857
Robert Schumann Haus, Zwickau

Three
CLARA SCHUMANN
(1819–96)

◆

In July 1839, when it seemed as if Robert Schumann and Clara Wieck would never be able to marry, he wrote to her:

> *Now all hope has disappeared. . . . All of this has affected me so deeply that if you had been with me yesterday, Clara, I would have been ready to put you and me to death.*

Now, if you had a boyfriend or girlfriend who sent you such an alarming threat, chances are you would steer clear. However, Robert and Clara lived during the nineteenth century, which is appropriately named the Romantic era. If every Romantic who vowed to commit suicide and murder over unhappy love affairs had actually gone through with it, hordes of Europeans would have dropped on the spot.

Although Robert's threat was idle, his letter did show his passionate love for Clara. It also revealed two other things, which she didn't see. First, her beloved Robert suffered from fits of severe depression, a symptom of mental illness. Second, in becoming his wife, Clara would have to make great sacrifices.

Clara Josephine Wieck was born in Leipzig on September 13, 1819. Her father, Friedrich Wieck, chose her name, which means "bright light." He vowed that he would make his new baby the greatest musician of her time. Friedrich was a self-taught musician who grew up in extreme poverty. He owned a piano store and gave piano lessons. Clara's mother, Marianne Tromlitz Wieck, was a professional singer and concert pianist. Friedrich demanded much of Marianne. She performed in concerts, ran the Wieck household, gave birth to five children in seven years, helped out in the store, and taught her husband's advanced piano students.

The Wieck household was very unhappy. Clara and her brothers were often left in the care of a maid, and received little affection from their parents. By age four, Clara had not yet spoken a word. Her father worried that his future musical star was deaf. He seated her at the piano and played a few easy pieces. Clara was able to play them back, note for note. She was not "deaf" to music—only to words. All she heard from her parents was angry talk, which she shut out of her mind.

All language sounded garbled to her until she was eight years old.

When Clara was five, her mother ran away from her father. Marianne knew that this meant she had to give up her children. Under the law of Saxony, children were their father's property, and Friedrich would get sole custody of Clara and her brothers. This caused Marianne great pain, but she could no longer bear to live with Friedrich.

Soon after Marianne left, Friedrich began to give Clara piano lessons. She took an hour-long lesson each day, followed by two hours of practice. Friedrich encouraged Clara to improvise at the piano and make up little pieces. He didn't think Clara needed much education besides her musical studies. A tutor came to the house only a couple of hours a day to teach her other subjects; all other children attended school all day.

Wieck thought exercise was important, so he started each day with a long walk. When his children reached the age of three, he required them to accompany him. He didn't slow down for the little ones, but expected them to keep up with him. Luckily, Clara could. In the evenings, Friedrich took his young daughter to concerts, plays, and operas. With such a busy schedule, Clara had little time to herself to read or play like other children.

Wieck was a ruthless taskmaster who was harder on his own children than on his paying students. Once he grabbed Clara's brother Alwin by the hair and threw him to the floor because the boy's violin playing didn't satisfy him. Another time he ripped one of Clara's favorite pieces in half and commanded her to practice only scales and exercises.

Wieck hated the idea of little girls performing in public just because they looked cute. He did not push Clara onto the concert stage too early, but had her perform in his home and at friends' parties. At each performance Clara played at least one of her own compositions.

When Clara was almost nine, her father remarried. His bride was a minister's daughter, Clementine Fechner. She didn't seem to mind that Friedrich took Clara along on their honeymoon to show off her piano playing. Clementine understood that Clara's career came first. Later, Friedrich would travel all over Europe with Clara while Clementine stayed at home. Clara never liked her stepmother and resented her presence in the household.

On October 20, 1828, at the age of nine, Clara made a brief first public appearance in a concert at the Gewandhaus, a prestigious auditorium in Leipzig. She played a duet with another one of Friedrich's young female students. Both Clara and Friedrich were favorably reviewed in the newspaper.

About this time, a handsome young man named Robert Schumann began studying piano with Friedrich Wieck. Schumann was an unwilling law student who dreamed of becoming a writer or musician. After working for two years with Friedrich Wieck, Robert begged his widowed mother to let him drop out of school and devote himself to music. Robert had played the piano since he was a child, but his mother felt he was too old to consider a career as a concert pianist. She wrote a letter to Wieck asking for his advice. Wieck, who was eager to get his hands on Robert's modest fortune, promised her that he would make her son "one of the greatest living pianists within three years." Twenty-year-old Robert came to board in the Wiecks' house at the time eleven-year-old Clara was preparing for her solo debut.

Robert was like a big brother to Clara and her brothers Alwin and Gustav. He made up tunes on the piano for them and told them scary stories. He dressed up like a ghost and chased after them, causing them to squeal in delight. Although Robert was much older, he knew how to act like a kid better than the Wieck children did.

At age eleven, Clara composed several piano pieces, which were published the following year. On November 8, 1830, she played her first public solo concert at the Gewandhaus. She performed some dazzling pieces and her own composition Theme and Variations. The Leipzig newspaper reported, "This young artist's extraordinary accomplishment, in her playing as well as her composing, led to general astonishment and the greatest applause." Robert was certainly happy for Clara, but he was jealous, too. Clara had made her debut, while Wieck was still assigning Robert finger exercises.

Robert suffered from mood swings. He would become very depressed, then very happy, then depressed again. He invented two imaginary friends, Florestan and Eusebius, to help him keep his emotions in balance.

Young children often make up imaginary playmates; however, it is rather odd for an adult to do so. Yet those who knew Schumann accepted his "friends" as part of a highly creative mind. Throughout his life he referred to them in his compositions, especially *Carnival*, Opus 9, for piano and in his writings about music.

In September 1831, Wieck took Clara on her first extended concert tour, traveling as far as Paris. Schumann was forced to end his studies with Wieck and to move out of his house. In Paris, Clara played many successful concerts. She met important musicians, including Frédéric Chopin and Felix Mendelssohn.

At Clara and Friedrich's homecoming party, Clara played Robert's new composition, *Papillons* ("Butterflies"), Opus 7. In the following weeks, Robert and Clara saw much of each other. They played piano duets, walked together, and flirted. They exchanged musical ideas and called their resulting compositions their musical "offspring." Clara was not yet twelve, but her concert tour had made her very mature.

Robert continued to practice diligently, but he began to doubt if he would ever become a great pianist. Sometimes two fingers of his right hand became paralyzed. This usually happened just before a performance, so it may have been a form of severe stage fright. Robert used a mechanical device that was supposed to strengthen his fingers faster than practice could. Instead, it caused permanent damage to his right hand. This dashed his hopes for a concert career. He was greatly disappointed, but also relieved. He no longer had to compete with Clara and other great pianists.

He could now concentrate on his composing and writing about music.

In March 1834, Schumann discovered a way he could earn a modest living in music. He and three other musicians started a publication called *New Journal for Music.* The journal included reviews of new compositions and performances. It would have a major influence on the music of the nineteenth century.

Clara continued to compose and publish piano works. Many of her early works merely showed off her fast finger work and are not important musically. "Soirees Musicales," Opus 6, however, is a collection of six short pieces that displays charm, warmth, and grace. It is similar in style to the works of Chopin, Mendelssohn, and Robert Schumann.

Clara's Concerto for Piano, Opus 7, is an amazing accomplishment for a fourteen-year-old, even though Robert Schumann supplied much of the orchestration. She uses some ideas in her concerto that were new for her time. For example, she didn't include pauses between movements; the entire work is played continuously. Also, in the slow movement the piano plays a duet with a solo cello in the orchestra. Robert Schumann and Brahms later used solo cello in their piano concertos.

Robert and Clara continued to spend time together. Wieck became concerned about the growing affection between them. He controlled all aspects of Clara's life, and he was careful to keep other men away from her. He dictated what she wrote in her diary or wrote in it himself, using "I" for Clara and "my father" for himself. He read her mail before she was allowed to. He always traveled with her and stayed in the same hotel room.

In April 1834, Wieck sent Clara to Dresden to study singing and instrumentation to help her compose for orchestra. This was also an effort to separate her from Schumann. The ploy worked. Schumann began dating seventeen-year-old Ernestine von Fricken, a friend of Clara's and a student of Friedrich's who boarded in his house.

Clara returned home in July for her new half-brother's christening. She was shocked to find that the child's godparents were Robert and Ernestine, looking very much in love. Robert noted in his diary that Clara looked "very sad," though he didn't seem to understand why.

Robert gave Ernestine a ring, which made them informally engaged. In September, she returned home to help care for her sick father. In her absence, Robert became interested in Clara again. For a while, he cared deeply for both young women at the same time.

In November of 1835, two months after Clara's sixteenth birthday, Robert kissed her passionately for the first time. The lantern she was holding "slipped" in her fingers. She nearly fainted. They were standing on her front steps, in full view of her father if he happened to be lurking at the window.

Yet Friedrich suspected nothing. After all, Robert was supposed to be engaged to Ernestine. Robert assured Clara that his relationship with Ernestine was over. He just didn't get around to telling Ernestine

Clara Wieck, age sixteen, with her own composition, Piano Concerto,
Opus 7, set on the music rack in the background. Lithography by J. Giere,
1835
Robert Schumann Haus, Zwickau

until January of 1836. When Wieck finally realized what was going on, he forbade Clara to see Robert and whisked her off to Dresden again. He wrote in her diary that Robert had treated Ernestine cruelly.

In February, Robert and Clara managed a secret meeting. When Wieck found out about it, he threatened to shoot Robert if he ever came near Clara again. Wieck demanded that she return all his letters. The dutiful daughter obeyed.

For a year and a half, between February 1836 and August 1837, Robert and Clara were separated by an agonizing silence. They never spoke or wrote to each other. Clara spent most of the time on tour, playing one concert after another. Robert composed furiously and worked long hours on the *New Journal for Music*. For all that time, neither Clara nor Robert knew what the other was thinking.

Finally, Clara could bear it no longer. She asked a trusted friend to deliver a message to Robert. Robert wrote back, asking Clara to marry him. The following day, August 14, 1837, Clara replied with a yes and the couple became secretly engaged, even though marriage seemed impossible. According to Saxony's law, a man and woman, no matter how old they were, needed the consent of their parents to marry.

Wieck was not about to give Clara up to any man. He didn't think of her as a separate person but rather as an extension of himself, like an extra leg or arm. He believed it was his teaching and his managing that made her what she was. In his letters he wrote about "our" concerts and "our" feelings. Her triumphs were his triumphs. Her piano playing made him a famous piano teacher. Her concerts made him a rich man, because all the money she earned was legally his.

Robert didn't seem to understand what he was up against. He wrote to Clara asking her to deliver a marriage proposal from him to her father on her eighteenth birthday. The idea terrified her. After having no physical contact with Robert for a year and a half, she now needed to see him face to face. They arranged a secret meeting. It was not as happy as Clara expected. The lovers felt awkward and stiff with each other. Yet they decided to go ahead with their plans.

Four days later, Wieck flatly refused Schumann's proposal, leaving Clara in tears on her birthday. Wieck argued that the marriage would end Clara's concert career. Her rivals for the stage—Anna Caroline de Belleville, Marie Pleyel, and Leopoldine Blahetka—all gave up their concert careers soon after they were married, and Wieck was certain Clara would, too. He had no way of knowing how committed his determined daughter was to her music. Clara's concert career would be the longest of any woman's in the nineteenth century, spanning over sixty years.

Clara dried her tears and wrote Robert, "Am I not a weak girl! I have promised my father to be happy and for a few years yet to live for art and for the world."

Off father and daughter went, on another long concert tour. In Vienna, where Clara had not yet played, she was a smash hit. The Viennese people jammed into the concert halls to hear her. A Viennese pastry was named after her: torte à la Wieck. The royal family

awarded her their highest musical honor, the title
"Royal and Imperial Concert Pianist." This was
astounding for four reasons: Clara was so young; she
was a woman; she was not a citizen of the Austro-
Hungarian Empire; and she was not Catholic.

Although it seemed hopeless, Robert and Clara continued their secret engagement. In the next two years,
they had to do a lot of sneaking around. Robert
addressed his letters to made-up names such as "BCDE"
and "Herr Kraus." Clara's friends picked them up at
the post office, put them in new envelopes—Wieck
recognized Schumann's handwriting—and mailed
them to her. Once, after a friend of both Robert's and
Clara's visited the Wieck's house, Clara was subjected
to an undignified body-search for a letter from Robert!
In order to steal a short visit with Robert on his twenty-
eighth birthday, Clara told him to come to her window
at exactly nine. If he saw her wave a white cloth, that
meant she would soon leave on an errand and would
meet him on the way. If he saw no signal, he should
go away without hope of seeing her.

Wieck was furious when he discovered that Clara
and Robert were still carrying on. He thought of a way
to teach his daughter a lesson. On January 9, 1839, he
sent her off alone on a long concert tour all the way to
Paris. Not only did he expect her to fail without him;
he wished for it. Paris was the capital of the musical
world. It was huge compared to Leipzig, with nineteen
theaters and three important concert halls. At first,
Clara was terrified to be facing it on her own. But she

had watched her father wheel and deal for so many years that she had learned the concert business well.

Once in Paris, she boarded with family friends, taught lessons, practiced, and arranged her concerts. She played several concerts, for which she received glowing reviews in the Paris newspapers. When these reviews and friends' reports of her success reached Weick, he flew into a rage. He threatened to disinherit Clara and keep all her earnings if she didn't give up Robert.

This time Wieck had gone too far, and Clara turned against him. She and Robert filed a request at the Saxon Court, for permission to marry without Wieck's consent. Robert sent her money for the return trip from Paris so she could appear in court. When Clara arrived in Leipzig, her father locked her out of their house, with her personal possessions and piano still inside. She went to Berlin to live with her mother.

What followed was a bitter court battle in which Wieck resorted to desperate measures. He broke into Clara's locked letter box and copied parts of Schumann's letters, in which Robert revealed all his weaknesses. Wieck accused Schumann of being a drunkard who was unable to make a living. He said Schumann had bad handwriting, could hardly speak, and was "a mediocre composer whose music is unclear and almost impossible to perform." He said Clara was not fit to be a housewife, since she had been raised to be a concert pianist and had learned nothing about housekeeping.

Wieck sent letters to concert managers, musicians, and music critics in German cities where Clara was about to perform, hoping to get them on his side in the court battle. In his letters, Wieck called Clara a "shameless girl who has opposed her father in the most unnatural and shocking manner." He warned other girls to stay away from her so they wouldn't be "poisoned." He also claimed she would ruin any piano she played!

No matter how badly Wieck behaved, Clara still loved him. Although she was never willing to give Robert up, she still suffered great anguish at being torn from her father. In her diary she wrote about his appearance at court:

> *He was so emotionally overwrought that the presiding judge had to make him stop talking, which cut through my soul each time. I could barely stand it, that this humiliation had to happen to him.*

Wieck couldn't get anyone to speak against Schumann. Even the jilted Ernestine stuck up for him. No musician wanted to testify against a music critic—that was bad for business. In the end, Robert and Clara won their case.

Friedrich kept all of Clara's earnings. She was embarrassed not to have a dowry "like any simple middle-class girl." She spent the week before her wedding playing concerts, trying to earn some money for Robert, who had supported her and her mother for the past year and had bought her a piano to practice on.

Finally, Robert and Clara's long, rocky courtship came to a joyous end. Two of the greatest musical

Robert and Clara Schumann in Vienna. Lithograph by Eduard Kaiser, 1847

minds of the nineteenth century were bound together
in marriage on September 12, 1840, one day before
Clara's twenty-first birthday. As a newlywed, Clara was
happier than she had ever been. Together the Schumanns kept a marriage diary, each taking week-long
turns writing in it. They played music together, studied
scores, and exchanged ideas about music.

Together they composed a set of songs, *The Springtime
of Love,* his Opus 37 and her Opus 12. When the songs
were published, Robert played a joke on critics who
were certain that a woman's compositions were inferior
to a man's: He simply wrote "by Robert and Clara
Schumann" on the title page, without indicating who
had composed which song. The critics couldn't figure
it out, even though Robert Schumann was one of the
greatest songwriters of the nineteenth century.

Clara's newlywed bliss soon came to an end. When
Robert composed, he shut himself up for long hours.
He rarely shared his music with her while he was
writing it. To make things worse, Clara couldn't do any
of her own work, because Robert needed complete
silence in the house when he composed. Clara had
worked hard at her music all her life. It caused her
great anxiety to sit idle. She wrote in her diary:

> *My piano playing is falling behind. This always happens when
> Robert is composing. There is not even one little hour in the
> whole day for myself! If only I don't fall too far behind. . . . I
> can't do anything with my composing—I would sometimes like
> to strike my dumb head!*

On March 31, 1841, six months after her wedding, she made her first public appearance as Clara Schumann. She was very nervous before the concert and feared that her audience had already forgotten her. But when she appeared on the Gewandhaus stage, the applause was thunderous.

At the time of this concert, Clara was three months pregnant with her first child. In the next thirteen years, she would be pregnant ten times and bear eight children: Marie in 1841, Elise in 1843, Julie in 1845, Emil (who lived only sixteen months) in 1846, Ludwig in 1848, Ferdinand in 1849, Eugenie in 1851, and Felix in 1854. Clara was pregnant or recovering from childbirth or miscarriage almost the whole time she lived with Robert. Women living in the nineteenth century didn't appear in public once it became obvious that they were pregnant. Clara, however, sometimes performed concerts one week before giving birth.

Marie's birth brought tremendous joy to the new parents. But as more and more little Schumanns arrived, Robert and Clara received them less enthusiastically. Robert suffered great stress worrying how he would support them. Clara wondered how she could possibly care for them all and continue her work in music.

Clara arranged a fifteen-concert tour from January 1 to April 25, 1842. It was not socially acceptable for women, even married ones, to travel alone, so Robert felt he had to accompany her. They left four-month-old Marie in the care of a wet nurse and of the family of Robert's brother Carl.

For Robert, the tour wore on and on, even though the concerts featured his compositions. He hated to travel; he was unable to compose; he worried about his child; and he disliked leaving his *New Journal for Music* in another editor's hands. The royal family in Oldenburg threw a party in Clara's honor; however, they neglected to invite Robert. She went to the palace and had a wonderful time, while he stayed in their hotel room and sulked. After that, Robert had had quite enough of Clara's concert tour. He returned home to Leipzig while she went on alone to Copenhagen.

This was a daring move. The journey to Copenhagen included an overnight voyage across the sea. Bad weather delayed Clara's crossing several times. She suffered the guilt of leaving her husband and daughter behind. Robert worried about her the whole time she was gone, and was so depressed that he couldn't compose. Clara's father, ever hopeful that the marriage would fail, spread the rumor that the couple had separated!

Two years later, in January 1844, Clara planned a four-month tour of Russia. This time there were two Schumann children, Marie and Elise, to leave behind with Uncle Carl. Robert didn't want to make the trip, but he reluctantly agreed, thinking they needed the money. He thought he would enjoy a break from the journal and he hoped to get some composing done.

Clara didn't mind getting up at three each morning so that they could be on their way at four, traveling by sleigh through deserted forests and over frozen rivers in the middle of a cold, cold Russian winter. She gave long recitals, without the help of other musicians, and was well received wherever she played. Robert, on the other hand, was sick and depressed the whole trip. He couldn't concentrate enough to compose, and wrote morbid poetry instead.

Soon after the Schumanns returned to Leipzig, Robert decided to sell the *New Journal for Music*, which was now ten years old. He was overworked and he wanted to devote himself full time to composing. This decision, however, may not have been the best one for his mental health. When Schumann composed, he worked night and day, at a frenzied pace, until he completed his project. Each composing session left him physically and mentally weaker. The journal gave him work to do in between compositions and connected him with the outside world. Without it, he turned his thoughts inward and became more and more depressed. Clara had planned another concert tour but gave it up to care for Robert. In August, he suffered a breakdown, which she described in the diary.

> *There were eight terrible days. Robert didn't sleep at night, his imagination created the most frightening pictures, in the mornings I usually found him bathed in tears, he gave up completely.*

In December, the Schumanns moved from Leipzig to Dresden. They thought the scenic hills and slower pace would improve Robert's health. During their five years in Dresden, Clara gave birth to four more children and gave fewer concerts. She supplemented the family's income by giving piano lessons. She composed most of her best works, including the Preludes and Fugues for Piano and Trio in G Minor, Opus 17, for violin, cello, and piano. Clara's trio was her most ambitious work and proves she had grown to be a mature, capable composer. She called it "effeminate and sentimental," but it is actually strong and energetic. Robert Schumann and Mendelssohn greatly respected it, and it was played often during the nineteenth century.

In May 1849, rebels revolted against the government, and fighting broke out in the streets of Dresden. The pavement and sewers were torn up and used as barricades during the battle. Cannons thundered and bodies were left in public view to warn the rebels against further trouble. But the rebels weren't ready to quit. They knocked on all the doors, forcing every able-bodied man to join their side in the fighting. Robert was anything but able-bodied, but they still wanted him. When they came looking for him, he hid in the house while Clara, who was seven months pregnant, made some excuse for him. When the coast was clear, she fled out the back door with Robert and Marie. She left her other children—Elise, Julie, and Ludwig, ages six, four, and one and a half—in the care of servants.

Clara, Robert, and Marie took the train for eight miles to Mügeln, then walked to a nearby village. From this distance they could still hear the cannons booming in Dresden. Clara suffered great anxiety about the children she had left behind, but felt it wasn't safe for Robert to return home. Two days later, at three in the morning, she set off for Dresden, accompanied by another woman. They valiantly trudged across open fields and encountered many armed soldiers who were tempted to shoot at anything that moved. The women reached the Schumann house, where they found the children unharmed, still asleep in their beds. Clara roused them, packed a few clothes, and was soon marching them across the fields to safety. Throughout all this, Robert shut himself up in his own creative world, and got lots of composing done.

In September 1850, the Schumann family moved to Düsseldorf, where Robert took the position of music director for the Düsseldorf Orchestra and Chorus. Robert didn't really want the job, but he felt the family needed the money. The workload was enormous— preparing ten full concerts and four church services a year. This, plus his endless composing, caused Robert great physical and mental strain.

Robert had little talent for conducting. He wasn't assertive enough to take command of a full orchestra. He spoke so softly that the musicians could hardly hear his suggestions. He gave them little instruction on how he wanted the music to sound. Clara, who understood Robert's compositions as well as he did, began to attend rehearsals to tell the musicians what he wanted. She worked as rehearsal accompanist for the chorus, calmly directing and supporting the singers from the piano. The musicians were amazed that such a great concert artist would take such a lowly position.

More and more Clara felt she had to defend and protect Robert, acting as a buffer between him and the outside world. While he appreciated this, it also hurt his pride and he lashed out at her. When she was practicing his Quintet in E-flat Major, Opus 44, he replaced her as pianist, explaining that "a man understands that better." He asked his assistant director to take Clara's place as accompanist at a choral rehearsal "since the piano drumming tired her and was more suitable for a man." He once called one of her performances "terrible," even though she played as well as ever. Clara wept bitterly and wrote in her diary, "If I did not have to use my playing to earn some money, I would absolutely not play another note in public, for what good is it to me to earn the applause of the audience if I cannot satisfy him?"

On September 30, 1853, a breath of fresh air swept through the Schumanns' strained household when a handsome twenty-year-old stranger with long blond ringlets knocked on their door. The man, whose name was Johannes Brahms, shyly asked if he could play the Schumanns his unknown compositions.

Both Robert and Clara immediately liked their young visitor and his music. Robert, who hadn't written any musical criticism for ten years, wrote an essay entitled "New Paths," which praised Brahms's fresh, bold style. He also helped him get his music published. Brahms visited the Schumanns almost every day in October. The three musicians played music and talked excitedly. These good times must have reminded the Schumanns of their joyful first months of marriage.

In November, after Brahms returned to his home in Hamburg, the Schumanns received a terrible blow: Robert was dismissed as music director. Clara would not admit he was unsuited for the job, and blamed the orchestra and chorus members. Robert wondered where he would find a new position after suffering such a professional embarrassment. He worried about supporting his family, even though he knew that three weeks of Clara's concertizing could earn an amount equal to his annual salary as a music director.

Robert grew more and more depressed. By February, he was suffering from hallucinations of sound. Sometimes a single note hummed in his ear, and other times a whole orchestra played music that he described as voices of angels. Sometimes the angels turned to demons or ghosts soaring over his head. He asked Clara to stay away from him, fearing that he would harm her.

On February 26, 1854, Robert asked Clara to take him to the insane asylum, because he could no longer control his mind. The following morning, Clara asked Marie to watch him while she consulted with doctors. Marie saw her father appear briefly in the hall, and assumed that he had returned to his bed. She then discovered that the back door was wide open. Alarmed, she called to her mother. Everyone began to search the house for Robert. He was out in the rain, in his nightshirt, crying, walking toward the Rhine River to drown himself. He threw his wedding ring in the river and then plunged in himself. He was rescued by some fishermen.

The doctors placed him in a private asylum in Endenich, where he had his own room, furnished with a piano. His confinement was surely the greatest tragedy of Clara's life. In her diary she wrote, "Him, the magnificent Robert, in an institution!—how could I possibly tolerate this!" She could not accept the fact that he had gone insane. She hoped that he had merely suffered another nervous breakdown and only needed a long rest.

In June, Clara gave birth to her last child, Felix. By October, she was still hopeful, yet uncertain if Robert would ever get well. The doctors advised her not to visit him, and she obeyed. She wrote him letters, and, when he was well enough, he wrote back. The doctors reported that some days he was calm, almost normal. But he rarely asked about Clara, and that hurt her deeply.

Many musicians offered to play benefit concerts to raise money for the Schumanns, but Clara insisted on playing her own concerts. She was too proud to accept charity—but, more important, she needed to work at music to ward off worry and despair.

During this time of Clara's greatest need, Johannes Brahms came to her aid. He put his own composing career on hold so that he could devote two years to helping her. He rented rooms in the same apartment house as Clara, played and discussed music with her, kept her household books, helped the servants baby-sit her children while she was on tour, and became her "best friend."

Johannes and Clara undoubtedly grew to love each other. Whether or not they became lovers remains a secret. They felt that their relationship was nobody else's business, and burned all their letters to each other. Clara willed her later diaries to Marie, who probably burned them; they are now lost.

Clara didn't see Robert for two and a half years. When his doctors feared he was dying, Brahms took her to Endenich for one last, heart-wrenching visit. The following day, July 29, 1856, Robert died of self-starvation.

Soon after, Clara and Brahms took a vacation together in Switzerland. They might have discussed a possible future together, although there is no record of such a talk. Clara may have had many reasons for not marrying Brahms, although we can only guess at them. She was fourteen years older than he, and may have thought she was too old for him. For her, married life meant bearing children, and she felt she already had more than enough. She took pride in the Schumann name and in the role of interpreter of her husband's works. Brahms was just starting his composing career, an occupation that usually made little money, and Clara had had enough financial struggles with her first composer-husband. Being a wife in the nineteenth century meant serving a husband, and Clara didn't want to obey or pretend to obey any man. Her concert career had been hindered by many obstacles during her marriage. She was now ready to pursue it fully and independently.

After their vacation together, Clara and Brahms went their separate ways. Clara faced forty years of widowhood; Brahms never married. Throughout their lives they kept in close contact through letters and visits, and remained "best friends." Brahms would die eleven months after Clara.

Clara worked very hard to support her children. She

provided them with food, clothing, the best schools, and a fine musical education. She saw them infrequently but managed them from a distance, mostly through letters. She met all their needs—except, perhaps, their emotional ones. Eugenie wrote this about her mother:

> Wherever she might be, we were ever conscious of her loving care, her protecting hold over us, and that to us little ones, as well as to the elder sisters and brothers, she was the greatest thing we possessed in the world.

Clara had made a lot of money giving concerts, so she could now afford to work less, but she found performing more fulfilling than staying home with the children. Once when Brahms urged her to take it easy, she replied, "My health may well be better preserved if I exert myself less, but in the end doesn't each person give his life for his calling?" She went on to say, "I . . . believe that a quieter life would leave me too much time to brood on my sorrows."

And Clara had many sorrows. She opposed Julie's marriage to an Italian count but gave her consent, remembering well the bitter struggle she had had with her father over her own marriage. Julie, who was weak and frail all her life, died of tuberculosis at twenty-seven, while pregnant with her third child.

Ludwig was committed to a mental institution at the age of twenty-two and spent the remaining twenty-nine years of his life there. His insanity brought back the pain Clara had felt when Robert suffered the same fate. She couldn't afford an expensive private asylum for Ludwig as she had for her husband, and she felt guilty that her son wasn't getting the best care.

When Ferdinand returned from fighting in the Franco-Prussian War, he was addicted to morphine, which he had taken to relieve the pain of severe rheumatism. He spent the rest of his life in and out of hospitals trying to cure his habit. He died at forty-one from the effects of his addiction, leaving a widow and six children for Clara to support.

Felix, the youngest Schumann child and the only one who never met his father, looked the most like Robert and inherited his talent in both writing and music. Clara, however, set such high standards for herself that she didn't expect her children to meet them and nearly discouraged them from trying. Felix's poetry was good enough for Brahms to use as texts for his songs, but when it came time to publish his poems, Clara asked her son to use a pen name in case his work wasn't good enough for the Schumann name. Felix was bitter that his mother had no faith in his talent, and his mother was hurt that he replied to her with an "unloving" letter. In the end, Felix had little time to prove himself as a poet. He contracted tuberculosis as a teenager and died at age twenty-four.

Marie, Elise, and Eugenie Schumann fared better than Julie and their brothers. All three became piano teachers. Marie never married; instead she remained with her mother, working as her assistant. Elise made her own career independent of her mother, married at age thirty-four, and had four children. Eugenie, who also never married, lived and taught with her mother and Marie for twenty years. At age forty, she went to England, where she was successful as a teacher and performer. Eugenie wrote a book entitled *Memoirs*, about her life in the Schumann family. She also wrote *Robert Schumann: A Portrait of My Father*, in which she quoted his diaries and other writings.

In her later years, Clara had many ailments, including rheumatism and arthritis. She suffered from shooting pains in her arms and fingers. By age fifty-nine, she had to rest for a week in between concerts. She also had hearing problems. She played fewer concerts and took a teaching position at the Hoch Conservatory in Frankfurt in 1878. That same year, she celebrated her jubilee—fiftieth anniversary—as a concert artist. Her musician friends surprised her by preparing a concert consisting only of her compositions, which they performed at Hoch Conservatory and at the Gewandhaus in Leipzig, where she had first appeared in public at age nine.

In 1888 her sixtieth anniversary was celebrated. She played her last public concert in Frankfurt in 1891, when she was seventy-two. Clara continued to play and teach the piano, and to edit Robert's compositions, until she suffered a stroke in March 1896. She died two months later, on May 20, 1896, while listening to her grandson, Ferdinand, play Robert's F-sharp Major Romance for Piano, Opus 28.

As a composer, Clara Schumann possessed great talent but not much self-confidence. Friedrich Wieck told her she could do anything as well as any boy,

Clara Schumann toward the end of her life
Robert Schumann Haus, Zwickau

including composing. Clara, however, thought her work was inferior, mainly because she was a woman. She wrote in her diary in 1839, the year before her marriage:

> *I once thought that I possessed creative talent, but I have given up this idea; a woman must not desire to compose—not one has been able to do it, and why should I expect to? It would be arrogance. Although, indeed, my father led me into it in earlier days.*

This sounds as if she was giving up; however, her husband, like her father, also encouraged her to compose. Clara wrote her best works after her marriage, but they never satisfied her much. Robert seemed to take more pride in her composing than she did. He put her original manuscripts in order and wrote out a title page and table of contents for the collection. He also arranged to have a number of her works published. After Robert's death, Clara stopped composing.

Clara Schumann is remembered more as a concert pianist than as a composer. She lived in a time of great change in the musical world. In the generation before her, the classical era of Beethoven and Mozart, pianists performed their own compositions. In Clara's time, making music became more specialized. Composers were no longer expected to perform their own works, and performers weren't expected to compose. Composing didn't come easy to Clara, as playing the piano did. She preferred to be an interpretive artist rather than a creative one, and felt that her most important work was to show the world how Robert Schumann's compositions were supposed to sound.

As Royal and Imperial Concert Pianist, composer, wife of Robert Schumann, mother of eight, best friends to Johannes Brahms, teacher, and editor, Clara Schumann managed to do it all.

Ethel Smyth. Photograph by Olive Edis
Impressions That Remained (*London: Longmans, Green, & Co., 1919*)

Four
ETHEL SMYTH
(1858–1944)

◆

When nineteen-year-old Ethel Smyth announced to her family that she intended to be a composer, her father just thought she had figured out a new way to rebel against him. Major General J. H. Smyth had good reasons to doubt that his spirited daughter was serious. England had not produced a great composer since Henry Purcell, born 199 years before Ethel. And, as far as the major general knew, there had not been any great women composers, in any country, ever.

J. H. Smyth began his successful military career at the tender age of fifteen, by enlisting in the Horse Artillery of the Bengal Army, stationed in India. At sixteen, he became responsible for developing roads, transportation, communications, and law and order in a large section of that country. He quickly rose to the rank of major general and drew a large salary. While on leave in England in 1848, he married Ethel's mother, who acted more French than English because she had been educated in France. She spoke five languages, played the piano very well, and had a beautiful singing voice.

Major General Smyth returned to India with his new wife, who gave birth to Alice, Johnny, and Mary, the first three of their eight children. The Sepoy Rebellion of 1857, when Indians revolted against British rule, made it unsafe for British families to live in that country. Major General Smyth moved his family to Marylebone in Kent, England, where Ethel was born on April 23, 1858. Later, the Smyths moved to Frimley, a village near London and Aldershot, where Major General Smyth became commander of an artillery depot.

Ethel's earliest memory was of jumping out of a low pony carriage as it slowly climbed a hill and landing on her back instead of her feet. In her memoirs, she commented: "Thus my conscious life began with the first of a long series of croppers—not a bad beginning."

Ethel best remembered her father dressed "in his Horse Artillery uniform with its masses of gold braid and shaggy busby," trotting off to the office, mounted on his tall charger, Paddy. Her mother often took a seat at the piano, pince-nez perched on her nose, playing dance music far better than all the other mamas, although little Ethel doubted that the other children could tell.

Ethel was the spoiled baby of the family for four years, until Nina came along. The births of Violet, Nelly, and Bobby soon followed. Big sister Alice was such a Goody Two Shoes that one nanny called her fine behavior "positively monotonous." She once pleaded to Ethel, "You have a very strong will; why not will to be good?"

For Ethel was always getting into trouble. She competed ruthlessly against Johnny, always trying to climb higher and run faster than he. One of Johnny's schoolmates promised to give Ethel sixpence if she rode a slim black pig named Fairylight. Ethel couldn't resist the offer, even though she happened to be wearing a clean, white, starched dress that day. Later she was involved in another incident concerning sixpence and a pig: She paid a farmhand that amount to let her watch him do the butchering. Ethel wrote,

> It was conduct which deeply shocked and horrified Johnny who considered such sights a male privilege. The terrific scolding that followed was unnecessary, since for months afterwards I turned green whenever I heard a pig squealing. At last even the nurse pitied me and would say, "Bless your heart, he's only squealing for his dinner."

Once when Ethel and Mary were very naughty, they knew their punishment would be to spend the afternoon locked in an empty attic room. Not wanting to be stuck up there with nothing to do, they snatched up as many books as they could stuff into their loose, billowy underwear, which buttoned up the sides. As the girls climbed higher and higher, their loads slipped agonizingly lower and lower. Just when their mother turned the key in the lock, their contraband boomed thunderously to the floor.

Ethel didn't get serious about music until she was twelve, when the Smyths hired a new governess who had studied at the Leipzig Conservatory in Germany. The governess introduced Ethel to many composers and taught her to play Beethoven sonatas on the piano. Ethel became a fine amateur pianist and had a strong singing voice, but her ambition was not to perform. She dreamed of becoming a composer, and began writing little pieces.

At age seventeen, Ethel took private lessons in harmony and composition from a local musician, Alexander Ewing. She became familiar with the operas of Richard Wagner by pounding them out on the piano with her teacher. She borrowed a copy of Hector Berlioz's *Treatise on Instrumentation,* one of the most important books ever written about orchestration, and taught herself how to write for all the instruments of the orchestra. Ethel's study with Ewing was cut short after only a year, when her father abruptly dismissed him because he didn't approve of him.

Actually, the major general approved of very little concerning his strong-willed daughter; yet he was quite liberal in his views about women in general. He noted that three-quarters of the land in their parish was owned by women, and therefore, he felt, it was unjust that women didn't have the right to vote in England. He budgeted his money carefully to provide an inheritance for each of his six daughters, so that none of them would be forced to marry against their wishes. Ironically, this gave Ethel the financial support she needed to rebel against her father and become a composer. She was the only one of the Smyth girls who claimed her money.

One evening at dinner, the Smyths began to discuss Ethel's coming-out party, at which she would be presented to society so that she could find a husband. Ethel calmly dropped a bomb on her father. She announced that no party was necessary since she was going to Germany to attend the Leipzig Conservatory, even if she had to run away from home and starve when she got there. Major General Smyth, who knew no artists and considered them all to be sinful, exclaimed, "I would sooner see you under the sod."

So began the greatest battle Ethel ever waged against the major general. She later wrote,

> *I not only unfurled the red flag, but determined to make life at home so intolerable that they would have to let me go for their own sakes. . . . Towards the end, I . . . refused to go to church, refused to sing at our dinner-parties, refused to go out riding, refused to speak to anyone, and one day my father's boot all but penetrated a panel of my locked bedroom door!*

Ethel sneaked into London to hear the few concerts the city offered. She financed her excursions by borrowing money from the village merchants, cheerfully telling them to charge it to the general. Ethel's father soon discovered what she was up to, just as she had hoped he would. She stubbornly argued, "You won't let me go to Leipzig, so of course I have to go to London to hear music."

At last, the major general gave in to his stubborn daughter, thinking she was doomed to failure and would return home again soon. On July 26, 1877, at the age of nineteen, Ethel set off to Germany, chaperoned by a brother-in-law.

In Leipzig, Ethel quickly settled into rented rooms. It would be a few months before classes at the conservatory began, but she was eager to hear all the music that the city offered. When she excitedly told her landlady about a concert she was planning to attend at an open-air restaurant, the woman explained that young ladies didn't go to such places alone. This didn't discourage Ethel. She donned a rented wig of gray corkscrew curls, a large pair of spectacles, a heavy veil, and a gown borrowed from her landlady, which she filled out with wadded newspapers. She painted wrinkles on her face and, at the restaurant, plopped a piece of knitting in her lap just for show.

Ethel spotted a housemate at the concert and decided to test out her old-lady disguise by shuffling up to him and asking him a question in a quivering voice. The young man didn't realize it was Ethel until the following day at lunch, when she asked him the same question in the same quivering voice, without wearing the disguise.

This was the only time Ethel bothered to keep up appearances. She went to any restaurant or concert she chose, alone and at night. Nothing bad ever happened to her, and she got to hear a lot of great music.

Ethel was on a tight budget. To save money for concert tickets, she often dined alone in her room, on a quarter-pound of cold ham, black bread, and beer. She kept her food cool and safe, locked inside a shiny new birdcage, which she set on the rain gutter outside her dormer window. A few cats tried to go after her ham, but the birdcage held fast.

At the Leipzig Conservatory, Ethel studied composition with Carl Heinrich Reinecke; counterpoint and harmony with Salomon Jadassohn; and piano with Joseph Maas. She soon became dissatisfied with the quality of instruction these teachers offered. She wrote,

> [Reinecke] was unable to conceal his polite indifference to our masterpieces, taking up his pen to resume his own before we had got to the door. . . . When [Jadassohn] arrived [for class], always a quarter of an hour late, it was to stand with his back to the stove for another ten minutes telling us exceedingly funny stories. . . . There was seldom time even to look at the work we brought, much less correct our mistakes. Maas was a conscientious but dull teacher.

Ethel was disappointed to find that her fellow students were not as excited about music as she was. Most of them had come to the conservatory merely to earn their teaching certificates. She did much of her composing on her own, mostly songs, piano pieces, and small chamber works. After a year, she dropped out of the conservatory and studied composition privately with Heinrich von Herzogenberg.

Heinrich and his wife, Lisl, introduced Ethel to
musical society in Leipzig, including their close friend
Johannes Brahams. In their letters to each other,
Herzogenberg and Brahms referred to Ethel as "our
little English friend." Ethel also got to know Clara
Schumann, and later met Edvard Grieg, Antonin
Dvořák, and Peter Tchaikovsky—all of whom respected
Smyth as a composer.

In 1878, Ethel took some of her songs to the famous
music publishers Breitkopf and Hartel. The business
manager, a Dr. Hase, told her that the only women
composers who had ever succeeded were Clara Schumann and Fanny Mendelssohn Hensel, and that Clara
was successful only because her music had been published together with that of her famous husband,
Robert, while in Fanny's case, her works had been
published under the name of her famous brother, Felix.
Dr. Hase added that Josephine Lang had written some
very fine songs, which Breitkopf and Hartel published,
but no one bought them. Ethel played her songs for
Dr. Hase anyway, and he said he would be willing to
take the risk of publishing them. But, after he had said
such hopeless things about women composers, Ethel
uncharacteristically lost her nerve and didn't ask for
any payment. She chided herself in a letter to her
mother: "Would you believe it . . . I asked no fee! Did
you ever hear of such a donkey!"

Of all the people Ethel met in Leipzig, Lisl Herzogenberg became her closest friend. Lisl had talked and
written much about her beloved sister, Julia Brewster.
This led Ethel to visit Julia in Florence in the summer

of 1882. Julia was married to Henry Brewster, an American-born philosopher and writer. Henry, whom Ethel called Harry, would become her collaborator, her best friend, and the love of her life. Harry and Ethel fell in love soon after they met, but didn't become lovers until after Julia's death. They then carried on their affair in a shockingly open fashion that caused one friend to ask, "Why don't you get married, and have done with it?" Harry's reply was "Because we don't want to have done with it."

On April 26, 1890, Ethel Symth's first piece for orchestra, *Serenade,* in four movements, premiered at the Crystal Palace in London, with August Manns conducting. Six months later, Manns also conducted Smyth's *Overture to Antony and Cleopatra.* By then, she was thirty-three years old, but a review in the newspaper called her "a promising young composer." Smyth's success encouraged her to write her first important work, Mass in D for Orchestra and Chorus, which she completed in the summer of 1891.

The Mass in D is a powerful work that shows Smyth's great ability for colorful orchestration. It is closer in style to the German composers Beethoven, Brahms, and Gustav Mahler than to other English composers of Smyth's time, Edward Elgar and Arnold Bax. Smyth's strong rhythmic themes and skillful use of development lead some musicologists to compare her Mass in D with Beethoven's *Missa Solemnis,* also written in the key of D. Smyth rearranges the order of the Mass so that her work does not end with the quiet prayer "Agnus Dei," but with the triumphantly joyful "Gloria."

Ethel Smyth always had trouble getting her works performed; however, she also had a talent for making friends, sometimes with people in very high places, and this is what helped her get her Mass produced. Ethel's friend Empress Eugénie of France offered to finance the performance. Another friend, Lady Ponsonby, asked her husband, Sir Henry, to speak about the matter to the Duke of Edinburgh, who made arrangements with the conductor Sir Joseph Barnby to have the Royal Choral Society perform the Mass at Royal Albert Hall on January 18, 1893.

But when Ethel attended the first rehearsal of her Mass, she began to have doubts about her work:

> *Never had I hated anything so much. All composers who have not yet arrived know what it is to sit helpless while your explicit instructions as to tempo, volume of sound, and everything else, are being brushed aside as irrelevant . . . and O! your timid attempts to modify the conductor's reading without putting his back up . . . terrible! terrible! But worst of all are upsurging floods of hatred for the work itself . . .*

Ethel discovered she had made a terrible mistake in orchestrating the "Sanctus" by giving the accompaniment of the singer's part to a quartet of soft brass instruments, which, to her, sounded like "husky mosquitoes." She wrote:

> *No sooner was the rehearsal over than armed with music-paper, scissors, stick-fast, and all the accursed paraphernalia of composers, I . . . re-scored the . . . Sanctus, as [if] it were at the cannon's mouth.*

This incident "deepened the gloom" Ethel felt about "the noises for which [she] was responsible." The standard of sight-reading was very low at the time, and she didn't have enough experience with orchestras to know that *all* first rehearsals of new works sounded awful. Ethel left the rehearsal thinking she was a horrible failure.

The final rehearsal of the program was scheduled for the following morning. The orchestra was supposed to practice George Frideric Handel's *Creation* at ten and Ethel's Mass in D at eleven. Ethel arrived at the Albert Hall at ten-thirty and got lost in the building while trying to find the door that led to the stage. She tore madly around and around the maze of corridors and up and down countless stairs. The sounds of the orchestra got nearer, then farther away, then nearer. Suddenly, Ethel heard "Exquisite orchestral sonorities."

"Ah!" she thought in misery, "*that's* how I'd like my music to sound!" Drawing even nearer to the stage, she heard a phrase that was strangely familiar. Abruptly she realized, "Merciful heaven! It was my own Mass!"

Ethel was so busy worrying about her Mass that she didn't bother to explain to her very proper father about her married boyfriend, Harry Brewster, who traveled to England for the performance and showed up at the dinner party given in her honor. She decided that "this seemed as good an opportunity as any other to bang together those two very *disparate* heads, Harry's and my father's." However, during dinner, Ethel noted that whenever her father looked in Harry's direction, "his upper lip rose slightly in a fashion that always reminded us of a dog who doesn't mean to fight, but now and again can't help showing his teeth. . . ."

Ethel believed that the performance of her Mass in D went very well. The audience received it enthusiastically and she was certain that it would be performed many more times. In her own words, "the Mass had come to stay." The following day she was shocked and sorely disappointed by bad reviews—what she called "the slaying of the Mass."

Ethel Smyth had a rare talent for picking herself up after falling on her face. She decided that the Mass in D received unfavorable reviews because she was not a member of England's "Inner Circle, generally University men, [who] . . . produced dull affairs." Of course they wouldn't accept a work "written by a woman who had actually gone off to Germany to learn her trade."

Ethel had to wait thirty-one years for the next performance of her Mass, which was presented in Queen's Hall on March 8, 1922, and received excellent reviews. The playwright and critic George Bernard Shaw wrote Ethel the following day:

> *Thank you for bullying me into going to hear that Mass. The originality and beauty of the voice parts are as striking today as they were 30 years ago, and the rest will stand up in the biggest company. Magnificent! . . .*
>
> *It was your music that cured me forever of the old delusions that women could not do men's work in art and other things. That was years ago, when I knew nothing about you, and heard an overture . . . in which you kicked a big orchestra all round the platform. But for you I might not have been able to tackle St. Joan, who has floored every previous playwright.*

Meanwhile, Smyth sought performances of her Mass in Europe. The summer after its premiere, she went to Munich and played parts of it to conductor Hermann Levi. Levi decided not to produce the work; however, he was so impressed with the dramatic element of the music that he told Ethel, "You must at once sit down and write an opera."

Ethel wrote six of them. The first two were *Fantasio* ("Fantasy") and *Der Wald* ("The Forest"), both with librettos by Henry Brewster. Henry wrote in German, because Ethel believed the works had a better chance of being produced in Germany: Very few operas were presented in England. *Fantasio,* a comedy in two acts, was produced in Weimar and Karlsruhe, in Germany. *Der Wald,* a tragedy in one act, was first performed in Berlin, Germany, in 1902, and then at Covent Garden in London three months later. The following year, Ethel Smyth traveled to America to be present when *Der Wald* became the first opera composed by a woman to be performed at the Metropolitan Opera House in New York City. After the performance, the audience offered her an ovation that lasted over ten minutes.

The Wreckers is Smyth's third opera and probably her greatest work. This full-length, three-act grand opera is her first major work that *looks* as if it was written by a British composer rather than a German one. The setting and characters are British, and the story is based on an actual incident in British history. However, the opera *sounds* German. Smyth's use of colorful orchestration and of leitmotifs—recurring themes that are assigned to individual characters and, in *The*

Wreckers, to the sea—show that she was greatly influenced by the German opera composer Richard Wagner, although she would never admit to this.

Smyth got the idea for *The Wreckers* while on a walking tour of the smugglers' caves on the Cornish coast. She sent Henry Brewster her notes; he then wrote the original play and libretto. The action of the opera takes place during the eighteenth century in a small Cornish sea village. The citizens there are religious fanatics who believe that God provides for them by crashing ships into the rocky coastline. On dark, stormy nights the people help Providence along by not burning a light in their lighthouse. They kill any survivors of the shipwrecks and plunder all the cargo.

The opera opens when the village has fallen on hard times because there has not been a shipwreck for a long while. The people believe that God is punishing them for their sins. Pascoe, the elderly village chief and preacher, urges his followers to go into the chapel to pray for a wreck. The chances are good, for a storm is brewing on the sea. However, Avis, a shrewd young woman, challenges Pascoe's reasoning. She believes that a traitor has been lighting a beacon to warn sailors away from the jagged coast. Thirza, Pascoe's young, beautiful wife, refuses to enter the chapel. She is revolted by the wreckers' savage ways and has rebelled against her husband by taking a handsome young lover, Mark.

Act Two of *The Wreckers* opens with an orchestral prelude, "The Cliffs of Cornwall," which Smyth also used as an orchestral piece, separate from the opera.

Mark arrives on the cliffs and begins collecting wood for a bonfire to warn ships. Thirza enters and begs him not to light the fire for fear he will be caught and punished by the villagers. Mark and Thirza sing a love duet in which they decide to run away from the village together. Moved by the passionate moment, Thirza lights the fire herself as a defiant farewell gesture to the wreckers. Pascoe enters to discover the bonfire—and Thirza standing in Mark's embrace.

Act Three takes place inside a cave that opens out to the sea, which serves as a courtroom for Thirza and Mark's trial. Avis, who is also in love with Mark, tries to save him by claiming that he spent the night with her, but no one believes her. Mark and Thirza are found guilty. They are left together in the cave to drown when the tide rises. The villagers leave the cave, singing a psalm for the dying. They lock an iron gate behind them, then head for the top of the cliffs. Mark and Thirza sing their last love duet as the waves rush into the cave.

Henry Brewster wrote *The Wreckers* in French, calling it *Les Naufrageurs* because a French conductor, André Messager, was expected to become the new music director of Covent Garden. Brewster and Smyth figured that using French would give them "the best chance of a performance in England of an English opera." Their plans fell through, however, and *The Wreckers* was never performed in the original French. Brewster translated it into German, calling it *Strandrecht,* for its premiere in Leipzig on November 11, 1906. Smyth translated it into English for its first production in England, under the direction of Sir Thomas Beecham at His Majesty's Theatre three years later.

Opera is always very expensive to produce. After the English production of *The Wreckers*, Ethel Smyth faced a debt of six hundred pounds. This was paid off by one of her most generous patrons, Mary Dodge, a rich American friend of Ethel's sister Violet. Mary Dodge also bought Ethel a small house in Woking, England, and provided her with an annual sum that Ethel called "a blessed difference to my income."

In March 1908, Ethel's beloved Harry was diagnosed as having cancer of the liver. His death, on June 13, left a tremendous void in her life, which no other man could ever fill. All of Ethel's other close friendships were with women. She wrote:

> All my life . . . . I have found in women's affection a peculiar understanding, [a] mothering quality. . . . It is a fact that the people who have helped me most at difficult moments of my musical career, beginning with my own sister, Mary, have been members of my own sex.

One of Ethel Smyth's passionate friendships was with Emmeline Pankhurst, England's most famous suffragette, who founded the Women's Social and Political Union (WSPU) in 1903. Between 1910 and 1912, Smyth put her composing career aside in order to help Pankhurst fight for women's right to vote in England. Her most important contribution to the movement was the composition "March of the Women," which became the official anthem of the suffragettes.

Ethel Smyth would often sing and play on the piano her entire operas in hopes of having them produced. Drawing by John Singer Sargent, 1901
National Portrait Gallery, London

Pankhurst was a dynamic speaker, who also drew attention to her cause by refusing to eat. Her dramatic hunger strikes often led the police to try to forcibly feed her. Pankhurst and her many followers were called militant suffragettes because they destroyed property in what they considered to be a war against the government.

The suffragettes felt they were gaining a little ground when the Conciliation Bill was proposed in Parliament in 1912. The bill gave a woman who owned a home or business the right to vote *if* a man didn't claim ownership of the same property. The bill wasn't much, but it was better than nothing. When it was ultimately defeated by a vote in Parliament, the suffragettes were so outraged that they planned a window-breaking rampage, which would lead to 150 arrests, causing the government great expense and inconvenience.

The one fault with this plan of revenge was that Mrs. Pankhurst was no athlete. Ethel, who once claimed that she might have been a more successful composer if she had not had "an inordinate flow of passion in three directions—sport, games, and friendship," volunteered to teach Mrs. Pankhurst how to throw a stone so that it would do some damage.

Teacher and student met for the lesson at dusk, near Ethel's house. Ethel piled up some stones and told Mrs. Pankhurst to aim for a large fir tree. Ethel wrote,

> One has heard of people failing to hit a haystack; what followed was rather on those lines. I imagine Mrs. Pankhurst had not played ball games in her youth, and the first stone flew backwards out of her hand, narrowly missing my dog.

Ethel instructed her pupil to move closer to her target. Even then Mrs. Pankhurst failed to hit the tree many times. With each failure her expression got

> more and more ferocious. and when at last a thud proclaimed success, a smile of such beatitude . . . stole across her counte-

nance, that much to her mystification and rather to her annoyance, the instructor collapsed on a clump of heather helpless with laughter.

However, the lesson didn't much help Mrs. Pankhurst's rock-tossing technique. When the women marched on Downing Street, the window selected by Mrs. Pankhurst "was duly bombarded . . . but the stones never got anywhere near the objective." Of course, Ethel hit the bull's-eye, shattering a window in the house of the colonial secretary, Sir William Harcourt.

Ethel Smyth was sentenced to two months in Holloway Prison, of which she served three weeks. Although she never got used to the "unpleasant sensation when the iron door slammed and the key turned," she did amuse herself by having tea in Mrs. Pankhurst's cell and leading the women in singing "March of the Women" while beating time on the iron bars with her toothbrush.

After her release from prison in 1912, Ethel Smyth returned to composing. The women of England were granted the right to vote six years later, in January 1918.

Needing a change of scenery, Ethel took up residence in a "harum-scarum but sympathetic and not too ruinous hotel" in Cairo, Egypt. There she set to work on a two-act comic opera, *The Boatswain's Mate*, based on a story by W. W. Jacobs with a feminist theme. In the overture to the opera, Smyth included her "March of the Women." "I simply stuck in the March because I like the tune," Ethel claimed in a letter to Emmeline Pankhurst. But actually she was more clever than that. She knew that audiences would recognize the politically significant "March of the Women," which would add popular appeal to her opera. *The Boatswain's Mate* is Smyth's first opera with an original English text. It is also similar in style to the light opera of her fellow countrymen W. S. Gilbert and Arthur Sullivan.

The boatswain is actually an ex-boatswain or ex-sailor, Harry Benn. He wishes to marry Mrs. Waters, a buxom widow and innkeeper, who will have nothing to do with him. Harry convinces an ex-soldier, Ned Travers, to stage a burglary at night in the inn, which Harry hopes will scare Mrs. Waters into thinking that she needs a man around to protect her. Harry's plan backfires when Mrs. Waters proves she is quite capable of taking care of herself. Armed with a gun, she locks Ned into a cupboard and is about to call for the police when he confesses to the hoax. Mrs. Waters releases Ned and they sing a funny duet: "Oh dear, if I had known he was quite a young man, I'd have put on more clothes!"

Mrs. Waters decides to teach Harry a lesson. She tells Ned to hide, shoots off the gun, and shouts "Murder!" Harry, who has been waiting outside to come to her rescue, dashes into the inn. Mrs. Waters horrifies him by singing "The first thing to do is get rid of the body." She sends him out to dig a grave, but since he is terrified of ghosts, he fetches a policeman instead, and together they return to the inn. Mrs. Waters produces the body, which is still very much alive and begins to woo her. At first she resists Ned's advances, but then decides to consider him as a possible suitor. It would be the best joke of all if Ned should become the lord of the inn instead of Harry.

In the first act of *The Boatswain's Mate,* Smyth uses spoken dialogue in between songs; however, in the second act, the dialogue is sung. Some critics complain that the two styles are too different to be used in the same opera; however, Smyth's plan is a good one for both musical and dramatic reasons. In the first act, much dialogue is necessary to introduce the characters and set up the fake burglary. If all of it were sung, the pace of the opera would drag. The second act consists mostly of action, and the continuous singing enhances the comedy of the situation.

While working on *The Boatswain's Mate,* Ethel Smyth met Captain George Hunter, who invited her on a camel-buying expedition for the Egyptian Coast Guard Service. The trek consisted of traveling into the interior of Egypt by camel, and then camping out until the camel dealers showed up with their goods.

Ethel and a fellow golfer on the trip, Gordon Morice, "did not see why [they] two should not knock up a nine-hole golf course somewhere." After camp was set up, Ethel and Mr. Morice "sallied forth" on their camels, accompanied by an orderly who carried staves, flags, and tin cups. Together, they assembled a nine-hole golf course, which consisted of one continuous two-and-a-half-mile sand trap. Ethel wrote:

Mr. Morice and I [had] thrilling golf matches, generally at cock-crow and both of us in pyjamas, gigantic Sudanese soldier-

*caddies handing us our clubs . . . in the style of acolytes handing
the sacred vessels to the priest at High Mass. . . .*

*I fell passionately in love with this life, the only drawback
being, at least during the daytime, the everlasting wind. But at
sunset it suddenly fell and then began the real life, the life with
the stars. . . . We all slept with our tent doors open and the
stars seemed only just outside.*

The arrival of about a hundred camels marked the
end of the ten-day desert adventure. Ethel returned to
Cairo and finished *The Boatswain's Mate*, then set out
for Vienna, Munich, and Frankfurt-am-Main to hawk
her wares.

To interest musical directors in producing her operas,
Ethel often sat at the piano and sang and played
through them in their entirety. Bruno Walter agreed
to produce *The Wreckers* in Munich, and *The Boatswain's Mate* was slated for a premiere in Frankfurt.
Ethel wrote, "My wild dream had come true; in the
coming winter two of my operas would be running
simultaneously at two of the first-rate opera houses on
the Continent!"

However, the outbreak of World War I shattered
Ethel's "wild dream." Plans for the productions of both
operas were canceled. She had to wait four years before
The Boatswain's Mate would premiere, not in Frankfurt,
but in London.

As early as 1913, Ethel Smyth had begun to hear
ringing in her ears. Five years later, she realized that
she was gradually going deaf. Unlike Beethoven, who
had a strong "inner" ear and composed some of his

greatest works after he went deaf, Smyth needed to hear what she wrote.

Probably for this reason, Ethel Smyth embarked on a new career in 1918, at the age of *sixty*. She became an author and wrote ten books. Ethel claimed she wrote for "Mr. and Mrs. Everybody." Her books are in a flowing, chatty style that is easy to read and highly entertaining. Smyth is also remarkably frank, a characteristic that was unusual for her time. Her writings include many vivid character sketches of famous people she knew as friends, including Johannes Brahms, Empress Eugénie of France, Sir Thomas Beecham, and Emmeline Pankhurst.

Most of her books, including *Impressions That Remained* (1919), *As Time Went On . . .* (1936), and *What Happened Next* (1940) are about her favorite subject: Ethel Smyth. *A Three-Legged Tour in Greece* (1927) is a travelogue; *Inordinate (?) Affection* (1936) is about her many large sheepdogs, nearly all named Pan; and *Maurice Baring* (1938) is a biography of that writer. *Female Pipings in Eden* (1933) is a very funny essay about a very serious subject: why women have not been as successful as men in the field of musical composition. In the opening of the book, Ethel Smyth wrote:

> One afternoon while Adam was asleep, Eve, anticipating the Great God Pan, bored some holes in a hollow reed and began to do what is called "pick out a tune." Thereupon Adam awoke; "Stop that horrible noise," he roared, adding, after a pause, "besides which, if anyone's going to make it, it's not you but me."

Ethel's career as a writer overlapped with her career as a composer. She composed two more operas, the "dance-dream" *Fête Galante* in 1922, which she later revised for ballet, and *Entente Cordiale* in 1925. She also composed Concerto for Violin, Horn, and Orchestra in 1927. As she fought increasing deafness, her composing slowed down and gradually ground to a halt. In 1930, she composed her last work, *The Prison*, for orchestra and voice, based on a text by Henry Brewster. In 1922, she was named Dame Commander of the Order of the British Empire, and afterwards, she used the title Dame Ethel Smyth. Four years later, she received an honorary doctorate of music from Oxford, after which she frequently appeared in flowing academic robes.

In 1930, after reading the feminist book-length essay *A Room of One's Own*, Ethel met and became close friends with its author, Virginia Woolf. The friendship was most unlikely, since the two women were complete opposites in taste and manner. Virginia admired Ethel's writing but disapproved of the way she wrote about herself in the first person with such rankling honesty. Virginia didn't understand Ethel's music, and Ethel was bewildered by Virginia's novels. Virginia was quiet and reserved, while Ethel shouted at the top of her lungs to hear her own voice, barged into Virginia's parlor unexpectedly demanding "to be seen," and hounded Virginia for advice about her writing, which she rarely followed. Yet the friendship survived and bloomed. Virginia wrote over three hundred letters to

Ethel and mentions her frequently in her diary. Here Virginia describes one of Ethel's visits:

> *In comes Ethel Smyth in her spotted fur, like an unclipped &*
> *rather overgrown woodland beast, species indeterminate. She*
> *wears, as usual, her 3 cornered Frederick the Great hat. . . .*
> *Before she has sat down she is talking. . . . [She drinks] not tea,*
> *no: but vermouth. "It won't make me tipsy?" [asks Ethel.]*
> *"Oh, I'm worn out." But she looks like a ruddy sea captain or*
> *old apple woman.*

Virginia attended a rehearsal of *The Prison* and wrote:

> *Ethel stood at the piano . . . conducting with a pencil. There*
> *was a drop at the end of her nose. . . . She sang now & then;*
> *& once, taking the bass, made a cat squalling sound—but*
> *everything she does with such forthright directness that there is*
> *nothing ridiculous. She loses self-consciousness completely. She*
> *seems all vitalised; all energised: she knocks her hat from side to*
> *side. . . . As she strides & turns & wheels about . . . she thinks*
> *this is about the most important event now taking place in*
> *London. And perhaps it is.*

In 1934, a series of concerts consisting of Dame Ethel Smyth's music was presented in London in honor of her seventy-fifth birthday. The composer viewed the festivities from the position of highest honor: in the royal family's box, seated next to the queen of England. Ethel sat proudly upright, looking attentive to the music, even though she couldn't hear a single note of it.

In summing up her life, Ethel Smyth credited all her

Ethel Smyth in her three-cornered hat, late in life. Photograph by Basil Fielding

The Letters of Virginia Woolf, vol. 4, ed. Nigel Nicolson and Joanne Trautmann (New York: Harcourt, Brace, Jovanovich, 1978). Used by permission of Nigel Nicolson

success to three attributes "that have nothing whatsoever to do with musical genius: (1) an iron constitution, (2) a fair share of fighting spirit, and (3), most important of all, a small but independent income."

A few months before her death, Ethel told her nurse-companion, "I think I shall die soon, and I intend to die standing up." She didn't quite, but she did dress and come downstairs every morning until her last illness caused her death on May 8, 1944, at the age of eighty-six.

Ethel Smyth was never satisfied with the few performances her works were granted during her lifetime. She hoped this would change after her death. She wrote:

> It amuses me to think that someday after my death, when all traces of sex have been reduced to ashes at the Woking Crematorium (so handy!) someone will very likely take me up as a stunt. . . . And thus, someday, I may make friends, musically, with those I cannot get at in my lifetime.

We are still waiting for *The Wreckers* and *The Boatswain's Mate* to join the modern opera repertoire so that we can all "make friends, musically," with this most amazing woman, Dame Ethel Smyth.

Amy Beach
Library of Congress

Five
AMY BEACH
(1867–1944)

◆

Many woman composers have had a hard time getting male musicians and publishers to take their work seriously. Amy Beach fought a different kind of prejudice—that of Europeans against Americans. It was a landmark victory for her when, in 1910, her compositions were performed in Germany. The orchestra members enjoyed playing her music and the critics gave her good reviews. "I was accepted not as an American, but as a composer," she announced proudly.

Europeans believed that America was a nation of savages, laborers, and gun-slinging rowdies. They didn't think Americans had the intelligence, sensitivity, or education to be accomplished musicians. Actually, it was the Europeans who were uneducated about America. They didn't know much about our country, so they made up wild stories.

This European snobbery caused many American musicians to suffer an inferiority complex. To measure up to Europeans, composers Louis Moreau Gottschalk, Edward MacDowell, Horatio Parker, and many others felt they had to study in Europe. But not Amy Beach. She was one of the first American concert pianists and composers to be trained entirely in the United States. She was an all-American girl who believed that all-American schools and all-American hard work would get her where she wanted to go.

Amy Marcy Cheney was born on September 5, 1867, in Henniker, New Hampshire. The roots of her family tree had been firmly bound to American soil before the Revolutionary War. Her father, Charles Abbott Cheney, graduated from Bates College and operated a prosperous paper-importing business. Her mother, Clara Imogen Marcy Cheney, was a pianist and singer. The Cheneys were quite wealthy and were able to provide their only child with the best of everything.

Amy showed a talent for music very early. At age one, she could sing forty songs in the same keys as she heard them. If anyone sang a song to her with a slightly different rhythm or melody than it had had when she first heard it, she complained that it was being sung incorrectly. Lively music made the little girl very happy, and sad music made her cry. When she was naughty, her mother punished her by playing Gottschalk's mournful piano piece *The Last Hope*. At age three, Amy began to make up little pieces on the piano. The following year, her mother wrote down the notes of her first two compositions, "Snowflake Waltz" and "Mama's Waltz."

Two years later, Amy began formal piano instruction, taking three lessons a week from her mother. She progressed quickly. After a year, she could play difficult pieces by Frédéric Chopin and Ludwig van Beethoven. She made her first public appearance at age seven, performing a Chopin waltz and a waltz that she had composed.

In 1875, the Cheney family moved to Boston, where Amy attended a small private school. She studied piano with three more teachers, including Carl Baermann, who had been a pupil of Hungarian composer Franz Liszt. At age fourteen, Amy studied music theory for one year. This was the only formal instruction she had to prepare her for composition. Anything else she needed to know she taught herself, learning through trial and error.

She learned counterpoint by writing out from memory nearly a whole book of piano pieces, Johann Sebastian Bach's *Well-Tempered Clavier*. This was an awesome task, because most of Bach's pieces contain four melodies played at once. It is extremely difficult to separate these melodies in the memory so that they can be written down one at a time. After doing this, Amy checked her work against Bach's to see if she had placed any notes in the wrong melody. By studying her mistakes, Amy discovered the rules of counterpoint.

She taught herself orchestration in a similar way.

When she attended a symphony concert, she listened carefully to what instrument was playing each part of the music. When she got home from the concert, she didn't go to bed, even though sometimes she was very tired and it was late. She sat up and tried to write down as much of the piece as she could remember, assigning each part of the music to the instrument she thought had played it. She then compared her work with the score, the written version of a musical composition. She also read—in the original French—Hector Berlioz's famous book about orchestration, *Treatise on Instrumentation*.

At age sixteen, Amy made her debut as a concert pianist, performing Ignaz Moscheles' Piano Concerto in G Minor with the Boston Symphony. The following year she played Chopin's Piano Concerto in F Minor with the same orchestra and the Felix Mendelssohn Piano Concerto in G Minor with the New York Philharmonic Orchestra.

A funny thing happened during the rehearsal of the Mendelssohn concerto. Conductor Theodore Thomas decided to give the kid a break by taking a slower tempo than usual for the piece, so that the piano part wouldn't be so difficult. However, after the orchestra played the opening measures alone, seventeen-year-old Amy launched into her first entrance at a lively clip, forcing the conductor to rev up the orchestra to match her speed.

In 1885, at the age of eighteen, Amy Marcy Cheney married Dr. Henry Harris Aubrey Beach, who was twenty-four years older than she. Dr. Beach was a prominent surgeon and instructor of anatomy at the Harvard Medical School, and an amateur musician who greatly admired Amy's talents. He was an important member of Boston society and good friends with the writer and physician Oliver Wendell Holmes.

Dr. Beach had a strong influence over his young bride. He urged her to leave her career as a concert pianist so that she could concentrate on composing. During her marriage, Amy rarely performed in public, except in concerts of her own works. She wanted to study composition, but her husband was against the idea. Dr. Beach felt formal instruction might take away the freedom and originality of his wife's musical style.

Both Amy's mother and her husband listened to her compositions while she was working on them, and offered suggestions. About her mother and husband, Amy wrote:

> [They were] the kindest, most helpful, and most merciless critics I ever had. How often they would make me work over a phrase—over and over and over!—until the flow of the melody and the harmonization sounded right! The result was that I had two critics before facing a professional critic.

Amy Beach described her husband as "old-fashioned." He believed a husband should support his wife. He insisted that any money she earned on her performances and compositions be given to charity. Many Boston hospitals and schools benefited from this arrangement.

Amy published all her compositions under the name

Mrs. H. H. A. Beach. In a music-magazine interview, Amy stated that her favorite thing to do after composing and playing the piano was to clean house! This sounds as if Amy was kept under her husband's thumb, but it wasn't so. Everything Dr. Beach wanted her to do was what she wanted for herself. Amy Marcy Cheney was a very determined young composer. She would never have become Mrs. H. H. A. Beach if marriage hadn't helped her reach her goal.

Dr. Beach did everything he could to promote and encourage his wife's composing. Amy Beach was one of the very few composers in all of history who *never* had to worry about money. Even Mozart, Beethoven, and Chopin had to teach to make ends meet. Also, unlike many women composers, Amy was never kept from her composing by the duties of motherhood: Her marriage produced no children.

Amy probably said she was just wild about housekeeping, and signed her compositions "Mrs. H. H. A. Beach," because she wanted to appear "ladylike." This was what she had been raised to do, and what society expected of her. Meanwhile, she competed in a man's world of musical composition, and succeeded enormously.

This was an amazing feat. Not only was it unheard of for a woman to compose music for orchestra; it was unacceptable for them to acquire any hands-on experience by playing orchestral instruments. Most young ladies played the piano a little, and a few played harp or guitar. The violin was out, since a woman's pretty face was distorted when she pressed her chin into the instrument. A woman clutching a cello between her knees was considered scandalous. A young lady blowing into a wind instrument or beating a drum was simply vulgar.

Yet some women broke the rules. All-women orchestras were a popular entertainment in New York in the 1870s. These "lady orchestras," as they were called, were viewed like the freak shows in a circus. It was not until 1900 that women playing orchestral instruments was acceptable to society.

Meanwhile, Amy Beach dauntlessly pursued her composition. Between the ages of nineteen and twenty-three, she labored over her Mass in E-flat, Opus 5, for orchestra and chorus. The Handel and Haydn Society of Boston premiered Mass in E-flat in 1892, the first time this prestigious organization ever performed a work composed by a woman.

Next, Amy Beach composed her *Gaelic Symphony*, Opus 32, the first symphony ever written by an American woman. Beach nicknamed her symphony "Gaelic" because many of its themes or melodies sound like Irish folk songs. When the Boston Symphony premiered the work on October 30, 1896, the audience applauded long and loudly. The American composer George Chadwick was so moved by the symphony that after hearing it he exclaimed, "Why was I not born a woman?"

However, the *Gaelic Symphony* received mixed reviews. Philip Hale, the music critic for *The Boston Sunday Journal*, praised Beach's symphony, stating that much of it "excites honest admiration." However, he complained that parts of it were "noisy rather than sonorous" and, in using too many instruments at once, Beach was trying to compose like a man.

The critic for the *Musical Courier* disliked almost everything about the *Gaelic Symphony*. "[It] is too long, too strenuously worked over, and attempts too much," he wrote. ". . . What she says in her work has been said a thousand times before, and better said." He stated that, in parts of the symphony, Beach wrote with "grace and delicacy . . . and there she is at her best, 'but yet a woman.' "

Therefore, the two main criticisms of Beach's symphony were that she composed too much like a man and that she composed too much like a woman! Yet neither bad reviews nor sexist comments discouraged Amy Beach. Soon after the premiere of the symphony, she set to work composing her Sonata for Violin and Piano, Opus 34. This was followed by another major orchestral work, the Piano Concerto in C-sharp Minor, Opus 45, in 1900. The Boston Symphony premiered the concerto, with the composer appearing as solo pianist. Beach then composed her Quintet, Opus 67, for piano, two violins, viola, and cello.

Besides these large works, Amy Beach composed many art songs and piano and violin pieces. She had a natural gift for melody; often her songs were quite easy for her to write. She told an interviewer from *Etude* magazine,

It has happened more than once that a composition comes to me, ready made as it were, between the demands of other work.

"The Year's at the Spring" was born [that] way. The Boston Browning Society had asked me to set that poem for their annual celebration of Browning's birthday. I agreed to do it, but put it off because of pressing work. Shortly before the celebration I went to New York, for the premiere of my Violin Sonata. On the train going back it occurred to me that the time was getting short for my Browning song. I did nothing whatever in a conscious way; I simply sat still in the train, thinking of Browning's poem, and allowing it and the rhythm of the wheels to take possession of me. By the time I reached Boston, the song was ready.

Nineteen ten was a tragic year for Amy Beach. She lost the two people whom she loved the most. First her husband died, and then, several months later, so did her mother. During her twenty-five-year marriage, she had composed most of her major works, with her husband and mother offering companionship and support. Amy felt such tremendous grief that she couldn't compose for some time and feared that her career had ended.

She thought that a change of scene might relieve her of some of her sorrow. She traveled to Munich, Germany, where she visited an old friend, Marcella Craft, an American soprano who sang in the Munich opera. Beach eased back into her career as a concert pianist by playing a few recitals for charity. She then toured with the Berlin Philharmonic, under the direction of Theodore Spiering, performing her piano concerto in Berlin, Leipzig, and Hamburg. She also performed her Piano Quintet with the Munich String Quartet, under the direction of the composer Richard Strauss. Beach then traveled to Rome, where she played her Violin Sonata and Piano Trio. She and her compositions were so warmly received in Europe that she was reluctant to leave. Her "short visit" stretched to three years.

In 1914, Amy Beach returned to the United States and settled in New York City. She divided her time between composing and performing as a concert pianist, although she sometimes felt torn between the two. Her practicing, traveling, and performing took much time and energy away from her composing.

Beach's reputation as a composer grew steadily. Her songs and piano music were especially popular. Around 1920, music teachers all over the country began forming Amy Beach Clubs, which were dedicated to performing her songs, piano works, and violin pieces. Everything Beach composed was immediately published, a highly unusual situation for an American composer. Beach became wealthy from the sales of sheet music, especially her songs. Her most popular work was "Three Browning Songs," Opus 44, which are musical settings of Robert Browning texts. From these three songs alone, Beach earned enough money to buy a summer home on Cape Cod.

Amy Beach knew that other women composers were not as successful as she was in getting their works performed and published. In 1924 she helped found the Society of American Women Composers, and acted as the organization's first president. The society sponsored many festivals that featured performances of music written by women composers.

Women who played musical instruments also had

trouble gaining recognition. Over half the music students in conservatories and universities were women; yet when they graduated, they found no positions open to them. The thirteen major symphony orchestras barred women as members (with the exception of harpists). Women musicians had to teach or accept lowly positions in ensembles that performed at restaurants, theaters, and silent-movie houses. This was especially unfair considering that most of the patrons and fund-raising volunteers for symphony orchestras were women.

Women musicians eventually gained some ground, but their progress was frustratingly slow. In 1925, the San Francisco Symphony hired four women string players, and between 1930 and 1940 three other orchestras hired a total of five other women musicians. Unwilling to let their talent go to waste, many women musicians formed their own orchestras. Between 1920 and 1940, nearly thirty all-women orchestras were founded in the United States. The most successful of these were the Women's Symphony Orchestra of Chicago, the Long Beach Women's Symphony Orchestra, the Cleveland Women's Symphony Orchestra, and the New York Women's Symphony Orchestra. Many all-women orchestras were directed by women conductors, who found it even harder to gain recognition than women players did. Some of the most famous pioneer women conductors are Antonia Brico, Ethel Leginska, and Elizabeth Kuyper.

In an *Etude* magazine interview, Amy Beach praised the all-women orchestras for making more of a contri-

bution to American music than the major symphonies
had. The latter still thought that great music was
written only in Europe; they rarely played American
music. In contrast, the all-women orchestras frequently
performed works by American composers, especially
women.

Although the all-women orchestras were greatly respected in the music world, they were still not of the
caliber of the major symphonies. They were so lacking
in funds that the music union had to make up a
separate pay scale, much lower than what other orchestras could offer their male members. Women musicians
demanded equal rights. They wanted better pay, and,
more important, they wanted a chance to compete for
positions in the major orchestras.

In 1938, the National Federation of Music Clubs met
in New York to discuss this issue. Sixteen women
orchestras, including over nine hundred players, clam-
ored for "mixed orchestras," orchestras that included
both men and women. The women demanded that
orchestra members be chosen by ability alone. They
suggested that all auditions for orchestra positions be
held behind screens so that the hiring committees
couldn't tell if the players were men or women. (This
practice was not widely used until the 1960s.)

The idea of the mixed orchestra was met with great
opposition, not just in the United States but all over
the world. English conductor Sir Thomas Beecham
made a callous joke about the subject. "Women in
symphony orchestras constitute a disturbing element,"
he said. "If the ladies are ill-favored [ugly] the men do

not want to play next to them, and if they are well-favored they can't."

The women musicians attending the 1938 meeting did not gain much ground. It took an international tragedy to open up the major orchestras to women. When male musicians were drafted to fight in World War II, the positions they left behind were filled by women. The women were then able to retain their newly won positions when the male musicians returned from war. When the best women players joined the major symphonies, they left large gaps in the all-women ensembles. Most of the all-women orchestras did not survive after the war.

One woman musician, Marian MacDowell, made a unique contribution to music in the United States. Marian was a concert pianist and the wife of Edward MacDowell, a composer and friend of Amy Beach. The MacDowells owned a summer home on a large piece of property near Peterboro, New Hampshire. When Edward died in 1908, Marian fulfilled her husband's wish of converting their home into a retreat for composers, artists, and writers so that they could create their works without being interrupted by the hustle and bustle of the outside world. Marian raised money by touring the United States, playing concerts of Edward's piano music, so that many private little log cabins could be built on her Peterboro property.

Between 1921 and 1941, Amy Beach spent nearly every summer at the MacDowell Artist Colony. During her visits there, she became close friends with Marian. Amy dedicated to Marian her *Three Piano Pieces*, Opus

128: "A Peterboro Chipmunk," "Young Birches," and "A Humming-Bird." At the colony, Amy also met and became friends with two younger American women composers, Mabel Daniels (1878–1971) and Mary Howe (1882–1964).

Amy Beach claimed that nearly every piece she composed after 1921 was inspired by her summers at the MacDowell Colony. One of her favorite stories was how she came to write *Canticle of the Sun,* for chorus and orchestra. In 1915, her friend Pastor Howard Duffield of the First Presbyterian Church in New York handed her a copy of St. Francis of Assisi's prayer "Canticle of the Sun" and urged her to set it to music. Amy promised to give it a try, but she was touring as a concert pianist and had no time to compose. She tucked the text away and forgot all about it. Ten years later, in June of 1925, Beach arrived at the MacDowell Colony with plans to write a long work for two pianos. She recalled:

> *I got out my manuscript paper and tumbled it upon my worktable. . . . I saw something fall from between the sheets. To my surprise, I found it to be the text that Dr. Duffield had given me so long before. I took it up and read it over—and the only way I can describe what happened is that it jumped at me and struck me, most forcibly! The text called melodies to my mind. I went out at once under a tree, and the text took complete possession of me. As if from dictation, I jotted down the notes of my "Canticle." In less than five days, the entire work was done. I put it aside to let it "cool," and the demands of the work I had planned to do crowded it from my mind a second time.*

> *Then, some years later, I was asked for a sacred work, the*
> *requirements of which . . . suited the work I had dashed off and*
> *forgotten. I got out my "Canticle" and did no more work on it*
> *than copy it out in neat and legible fashion . . . and there was*
> *the work, as it is known today.*

Beach's *Canticle of the Sun* was enormously popular and received many performances. Some musical organizations performed it annually, just as many ballet companies perform *The Nutcracker Suite* every Christmas.

In 1932, at the very late age of sixty-five, Beach decided to tackle the monumental chore of composing an opera. Her work *Cabildo* is about a swashbuckling hero, Pierre Lafitte, who escapes from the Cabildo prison in New Orleans during the War of 1812. Lafitte falls in love with a mysterious lady who washes up soaking wet from a shipwreck. The greatest moments in the opera come when the swashbuckler and his soggy girlfriend sing a couple of rapturous love duets that can easily cause a flood of tears in an audience. The corny libretto, by Nan Bagby Stephens, may have been why the opera was a flop. *Cabildo* received one performance in the 1940s at the University of Georgia and another one, thirty years later, at the Missouri–Kansas City Conservatory.

Many opera composers wrote a number of failures before coming up with a winner. Considering how gifted Beach was at songwriting, she might have composed a great opera if she had started working at the form at a younger age and acquired enough experience in theater to choose better dramatic material.

In 1938, Beach composed her last large work, the
impressive Piano Trio in A Minor, Opus 150, for
violin, cello, and piano. At age seventy-four, when she
departed for the MacDowell Colony, the *Musical Courier* reported that "she is still alert to the opportunities
of composition." This was to be her last visit to the
MacDowell Colony to write her last compositions.
Amy Beach died of heart disease three years later, on
December 27, 1944, in New York City. She had written
over three hundred works and nearly every type of
composition.

To understand Amy Beach's place in musical history,
we have to take a look at the rest of the musical world.
While she was growing up, she was inspired by the
great Romantic composers writing at that time: Richard Wagner, Johannes Brahms, Edvard Grieg, Claude
Debussy, and Edward MacDowell. Beach drew much of
her own musical language from these composers and
continued to write in a Romantic style throughout her
long life. Like Sergey Rachmaninoff, she chose to write
in a nineteenth-century style during the twentieth
century.

Meanwhile, twentieth-century composers such as
Arnold Schoenberg, Charles Ives, Béla Bartók, and
Igor Stravinsky were exploring startling new ways to
make music. Old, Romantic styles were pushed aside
to make way for new, modern techniques. By the end
of her life, Amy Beach still had many fans who loved
her dearly, and enthusiastically performed her music.
Even so, musicologists dismissed her music as being
overly sentimental, old-fashioned, and merely woman's

work. After Beach died, her piano music and songs went out of print and no orchestras performed her symphony and concerto. It seemed as if her music had died with her.

But recently musicologists have given Amy Beach's work a second look. After careful consideration, they have discovered that her unique style deserves more recognition. Currently there is an Amy Beach revival; her works are being performed, published, and recorded. Perhaps one day you will attend a concert and hear music by Amy Beach—noted composer and all-American girl.

Florence Price
Used by permission of the University of Arkansas Library

Six
FLORENCE PRICE
(1888–1953)

◆

On April 9, 1888, only twenty-three years after the Emancipation Proclamation freed the slaves, a black girl possessing great talents was born in Little Rock, Arkansas. The baby's name was Florence Beatrice Smith, but she would later become known to the world by her married name, Florence Price. As a young girl, Florence dreamed of becoming a medical doctor. However, she thought that girls, especially black girls, couldn't become doctors. So she decided to be a composer. It didn't seem to bother her that women had even less opportunity in this profession. Florence Price became the first black woman and the second black person to compose a symphony that was performed by a major orchestra.

Her father was Dr. James H. Smith, the first black dentist to have an office on Main Street in Little Rock. He was also a painter, a politician, a novelist, and an inventor, who drew royalties for his inventions. He was a kind, well-liked man, known for his fairness. Once, when both a cleaning woman and the governor of Arkansas were in the waiting room of his dental office, he attended to the cleaning woman first, because she had been waiting longer.

Florence's mother, Florence Irene Gulliver Smith, was of both black and white ancestry. Her family was quite wealthy and owned a large amount of land. Her father, who was a barber, owned a chain of barbershops. Mrs. Smith was an elementary school teacher who sang and played the piano. She and James Smith had two children older than Florence: Charles and Gertrude.

Little Florence began taking piano lessons from her mother at a very young age. She composed her first piano pieces and performed them in a public recital at the age of four. She wrote her first published composition when she was eleven. Later, she studied organ and violin.

During Florence's childhood, whites in Arkansas were very prejudiced against blacks. Starting in 1888, the year of Florence's birth, the number of blacks holding public office began to diminish. By 1894, blacks no longer held any seats in either house of the legislature. In 1906, white lawmakers robbed blacks of their right to vote by establishing the all-white primary election. Black children were not allowed to go to school with white children, so Florence attended a public elementary school for blacks only. (Another black composer, William Grant Still, born in 1895, would later attend the same school.)

Florence attended Capitol High School, also in Little Rock. In 1903, at the young age of fourteen, she became valedictorian of her graduating class. Florence and her mother then moved to Boston so that she could attend the New England Conservatory, one of the best music schools in America.

Mrs. Smith was afraid that Florence would encounter more racial prejudice in college and would miss out on professional opportunities just because she was black, so she tried to pass Florence off as Mexican by stating on her application form that her birthplace was Pueblo, Mexico. Mrs. Smith rented an expensive apartment and hired a full-time maid so it would appear that she and her daughter were members of high society. When Florence was asked to be a bridesmaid, Mrs. Smith embarrassed her by making her wear a lavish dress embroidered with seed pearls, which was far more expensive than the bride could afford.

Florence felt bitter toward her mother even though Mrs. Smith was doing what she thought was best for her. Florence wanted to admit to her Little Rock birthplace and just be herself. She thought her mother was ashamed of the black part of her heritage. Perhaps this is true, because after her husband died, Mrs. Smith burned the pictures and records of her life with him in Little Rock and went to live with her white relatives.

By joining the ranks of whites, she was probably trying to avoid the suffering they caused blacks.

Blacks, however, were treated better in Boston than they were in Little Rock. The New England Conservatory accepted black students, although at the time very few were enrolled there. One black woman was in the graduating class a year ahead of Florence's, and another black student was in Florence's class. William Grant Still attended New England Conservatory a few years after Florence.

Florence studied composition with the American composers George Chadwick and Frederick Converse, who were well known at the time. Chadwick used the nineteenth-century musical concept of nationalism in many of his compositions. Nationalistic composers use folk songs, dances, legends, and landscapes of their homeland in their compositions. Czech composer Bedřich Smetana wrote an orchestral work called *The Moldau* about an important river running through Czechoslovakia, and Russian composer Modest Mussorgsky wrote an opera called *Boris Godunov* about the czar of that name. In his compositions, Chadwick used some material taken from African-American music, and he probably encouraged Florence to do the same.

Florence Price also became a nationalistic composer, applying elements of African-American music in almost all her works. Throughout her life, she would compose as Chadwick taught her, combining nationalism, nineteenth-century harmony, and traditional classical form. While studying with Chadwick, Florence wrote a string trio for violin, viola, and cello, and a symphony.

Florence performed on both organ and piano in recitals at the New England Conservatory. She won an organ-playing competition at a prestigious church in nearby Nantucket and performed in a place of honor in her senior-class concert. After three years of study, she graduated in 1906, at the age of eighteen, with a diploma in organ performance and a teaching certificate in piano.

Florence returned home to begin her teaching career. She took a position on the music faculty at Shorter College in North Little Rock. Her parents had separated by then and she kept house for her father. In 1910, she became the head of the music department at Clark College in Atlanta, Georgia. She returned to Little Rock two years later to marry a young lawyer, Thomas J. Price.

Price had been a lawyer at the Scipio Africanus Jones law firm for four years. In 1919, Jones and the other lawyers in his firm began a four-year court battle known as the Elaine Race Riot Case. They defended some black men who had been involved in the riot and faced possible death sentences. Jones and his associates accomplished the incredible feat of saving these black men's lives in a prejudiced court. In 1923, Price left Jones to establish his own law office.

Meanwhile, Florence composed; taught private lessons in piano, organ, and violin; and raised a family. The Prices' first child was a son, Tommy, who died as

an infant. Florence Louise was born in 1917, and Edith
was born in 1921.

Soon after Tommy's death, Florence composed the
art song "To My Little Son," using this poem by Julia
Johnson Davis:

> *In your face I sometimes see*
> *Shadowings of the man to be*
> *And eager dream of what my son shall be*
> *In twenty years and one*
>
> *When you are to manhood grown*
> *And all your manhood ways are known,*
> *Then shall I, wistful, try to trace*
> *The child you once were in your face.*

It must have been painful for Florence to set these
words to music, while knowing she would never see her
own little son grow up; but she wanted to keep his
memory alive in a composition she wrote.

Price composed many other art songs and arranged
many black spirituals. Black spirituals are religious
American folk songs that were sung by the slaves and,
later, in the black churches of the South. Price became
well known as a composer of art songs later in her life,
when two famous black opera singers, Marian Anderson and Leontyne Price (no relation to Florence),
performed and recorded her works.

Florence Price's most famous songs are "My Soul's
Been Anchored in the Lord," an arrangement of a
black spiritual, and "Songs to a Dark Virgin," a musical
setting of a poem with the same title written by black
poet Langston Hughes. The first time Marian Ander-

son performed "Songs to a Dark Virgin," the reviewer for the *Chicago Daily News* described it as "one of the greatest immediate successes ever won by an American song." Afterwards, four music publishers vied for rights to publish this song.

While living in Little Rock, Florence Price and her family came up against much racial prejudice. The Arkansas Music Teachers Association would not allow Florence to become a member because she was black. In 1927, a black man who was accused of attacking a white woman was hanged by a gang of white men from a tree in a middle-class black neighborhood. This terrorist act caused many professional black families, including the Prices, to move out of Little Rock.

The Prices settled in Chicago, where Florence continued to compose, perform, and teach. She also continued her own education, attending classes at the Chicago Musical College, Chicago Teachers College, Chicago University, and the Lewis Institute. She studied composition at the American Conservatory of Music with Leo Sowerby, a composer known for his organ and church music, who won the Pulitzer Prize in music in 1946 for *The Canticle of the Sun.*

Florence Price wanted her works performed on the concert stage, and she wanted them published so she could earn an income from royalties. However, she soon learned, like many other composers, that publishers wanted works that would sell many copies. This led Price to compose two types of music: serious, sophisticated works for the concert stage; and teaching pieces for sheet-music publishers to sell to piano students.

Without telling Florence, in 1928, Thomas Price entered her piano solo "Cotton Gin" in a contest sponsored by G. Schirmer Music Publishers. Florence was very surprised when she won first prize. "Cotton Gin" was published by Schirmer and she received a royalty contract for it. At this time, McKinley Publishing Company also began publishing her piano pieces for students.

"The Old Boatman" and some of Price's other piano pieces are very easy, while "Arkansas Jitter," *Three Little Negro Dances, Dances of the Canebrakes,* and other works are geared for the more advanced pianist. In these pieces, Price uses material taken from African-American folk songs and dance. She doesn't use actual folk tunes but instead makes up her own melodies based on traditional African-American music.

Price, however, does use authentic African-American rhythms. In her program notes for *Three Little Negro Dances,* Price wrote that rhythm was the "compelling, onward-sweeping force" in African-American dance. She also pointed out that rhythm was an important element in all African-American activity, including work, play, singing, and praying.

Dances of the Canebrakes is a suite—a set of short pieces about the same subject matter. It consists of three movements: "Nimble Feet," "Tropical Noon," and "Silk Hat and Walking Cane." "Nimble Feet" is a collection of short musical ideas, connected by a steady, pulsing beat. Some of these ideas sound similar to the music of Scott Joplin, George Gershwin, and Chuck Berry. What we hear is not a copy of these other composers' works but rather the elements of African-American folk music present in all of them. "Tropical Noon" is a lazy, mellow movement, which reminds us how hard it is to move fast on a hot, sultry day. It shows off Florence Price's gift for writing melody. "Silk Hat and Walking Cane" is a laid-back two-step similar to ragtime, when ragtime is played correctly at a slower tempo than we usually hear.

In Chicago, Florence became friends with a musician named Mrs. Estella C. Bonds. Mrs. Bonds opened her home to many black artists, including sculptor Richmond Barthé, poet Langston Hughes, and singer-actress Abbie Mitchell. Mrs. Bonds' daughter, Margaret, born in 1913, was a talented concert pianist and composer. She studied composition with Florence Price and became her most famous pupil.

The depression of the 1930s made it especially hard for artists to make a living. Florence taught as much as she could, but in 1931, she was laid up with a broken foot. This gave her time to work on her Symphony in E Minor. In a letter to a friend, she wrote, "I found it possible to snatch a few precious days in the month of January in which to write undisturbed, but oh, dear me, when shall I ever be so fortunate again as to break a foot."

Florence had so little income that Estella Bonds invited her and her family to come live in her house so that she wouldn't have to worry about money for a while. On cold winter nights, the two composers, Florence Price and Margaret Bonds, worked at the large kitchen table, music paper strewn all around them. Florence copied out her symphony, preparing a part for each section of the orchestra to play. The women were getting their compositions ready to enter a contest sponsored by the Rodman Wanamaker Foundation. The 1932 Wanamaker Awards offered a total of $1,000 in prizes—money both composers needed badly.

Their hard work was greatly rewarded. Price won the $500 first prize in the symphonic music category for her Symphony No. 1 in E Minor and the $250 first prize in the solo competition category for her Piano Sonata in E Minor. Bonds won the $250 first prize in the art song category, for "The Sea Ghost."

In her symphony, Price combines elements of African-American music with the form and composing techniques of classical music. The second of the four movements captures the mood of the black spiritual. The third movement contains material taken from the juba, a black folk dance developed by slaves but not performed onstage until the late 1800s. The juba is in duple meter and its tempo is fast. Many of the rhythms are syncopated, meaning that accented notes pop out of the music unexpectedly. Price uses noisemakers such as cowbells, tin pans, and squeals to emphasize the joyous, high-spirited mood of the juba.

Frederick Stock, the conductor of the Chicago Symphony, became interested in Florence Price's award-winning symphony. He arranged a performance of it for June 15, at the 1933 Chicago World's Fair "Century of Progress Exposition." The performance was heard all over the nation on a live radio broadcast, aired by Columbia Broadcasting. This made Florence Price the first black woman composer and the second black composer to have a symphony performed by a major orchestra. (William Grant Still's *Afro-American Symphony* had been played by the Rochester Symphony, under the direction of Howard Hanson, two years earlier.)

In a review in the *Chicago Daily News*, Price's Symphony No. 1 in E Minor was called "a faultless work . . . a work that speaks its own message with restraint and yet with passion. Mrs. Price's symphony is worthy of a place in the regular symphonic repertoire."

Many performances of Florence Price's symphony followed the first one. During the World's Fair, the Illinois Host House, on the exposition grounds, presented Price in a program of her own compositions; the International Council of Women invited her to appear on a program of original compositions by women; and the Women's Symphony Orchestra of Chicago performed her Piano Concerto No. 1 in F Minor, with Ebba Sundstrum conducting and Price playing the solo piano part. In the summer of 1935, the Women's Symphony Orchestra of Chicago performed the concerto again, featuring Florence Price as the conductor and her student Margaret Bonds as the piano soloist. This concerto was also performed by the Chicago Symphony, featuring Price as the pianist.

In 1935, Florence Price returned to Little Rock to perform a concert of her own music. By then she was so well known that a brass band offered to meet her at the train station. She asked the band not to come, since so much noisy attention would embarrass her. The two Little Rock newspapers, the *Arkansas Gazette*

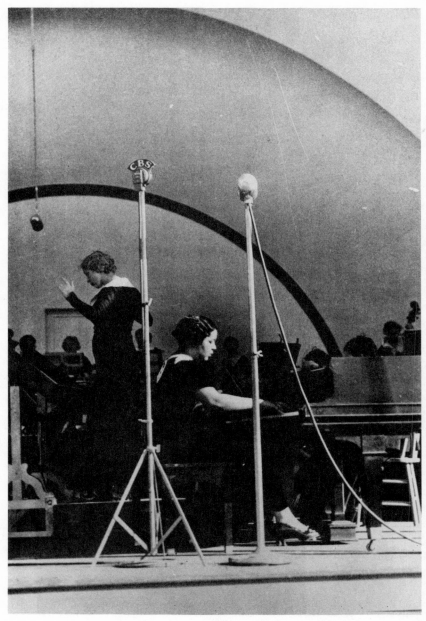

Florence Price conducts the Women's Symphony Orchestra of Chicago in a performance of her Piano Concerto No. 1 in F Minor, with Margaret Bonds appearing as soloist
Used by permission of the University of Arkansas Library

and the *Arkansas Democrat,* published articles announcing Price's concert. Oddly, the articles didn't mention that Price was a native of Little Rock; however, they did state that "seats will be reserved for white people." Apparently, Little Rock hadn't changed much since Price lived there.

A review in the black newspaper *Arkansas Survey Journal* stated that Price was "a noted musician of Chicago," who "thrilled a magnificent audience of eager listeners. . . . All of Little Rock turned out to hear [her] and sat spellbound throughout the entire performance."

On November 6, 1940, Price's Symphony No. 3 in C Minor was performed by the Michigan WPA Symphony in Detroit, under the direction of Valter Poole. On the same program, Price appeared as the piano soloist in her Piano Concerto No. 2 in D Minor.

Eleanor Roosevelt attended the rehearsal of this program, and was so impressed by Price's music that she canceled her previous engagements so she could go to the performance. In the November 14 installment of her newspaper column, "My Day," Roosevelt wrote that Florence Price was "one of the few women to write symphonic music . . . who has certainly made a contribution to our music. The orchestra rendered her symphony beautifully."

Sir John Barbirolli, a British conductor, asked Price to write a piece for string orchestra. She responded by composing *Suite of Negro Dances,* presented by Barbirolli in Manchester, England. (A performance of the same work by the Chicago Symphony was aired on

February 18, 1953, by Chicago WGN-TV, as part of
its series *Television "Pops" Concerts.*

Price's works were also performed by the Detroit
Symphony, the Brooklyn Symphony, the Bronx Sym-
phony, the Pittsburgh Symphony, the New York City
Symphonic Band, and the United States Marine Band.
Her music has been performed in France, Germany,
Canada, England, Switzerland, Mexico, and Austria.
Price's other orchestral works include *Concert Over-
tures,* premiered by the American Symphony Orches-
tra; *Abraham Lincoln Walks at Midnight,* a work for
orchestra, chorus, and organ; and two violin concertos.

Florence Price became a widow in 1942. She continued teaching and composing, and kept up with many
other activities. Her hobbies included painting china
and reading medical journals, since her interest in
medicine continued throughout her life. She attended
the Presbyterian church. She wrote many letters to
friends, musicians, and music publishers and kept a
daily diary in which she recorded her activities and
notated musical ideas. Once when she was writing in
her diary, a bird outside her window attracted her
attention. She wrote, "A bird [is] now singing this
phrase over and over," and then notated the bird's
song.

Florence Price was a member of many professional
organizations, including the American Society of
Composers, Authors, and Publishers (ASCAP). Perhaps her favorite organization was the Chicago Club of
Women Organists. Price wrote many compositions for
organ, which she and other members of the Chicago
Club of Women Organists presented in recitals.

In 1951, Price's *Sea Gulls,* a composition for women's chorus, won first prize in a contest sponsored by the Lake View Music Society. Her many other works for chorus include *Song for Snow* and *Moon Bridge.* Her chamber works include string quartets, two quintets for piano and strings, and *Moods* for flute, clarinet, and piano.

In the spring of 1953, when Florence Price began making arrangements for a trip to Europe, she suddenly became ill. After a brief stay in St. Luke's Hospital in Chicago, she died on June 3.

Eleven years later, on November 24, 1964, an elementary school in Chicago was named the Florence B. Price School in her honor. The dedication ceremony featured performances of her Piano Concerto No. 1 and Violin Concerto No. 2, and the second-grade class sang her song "It's Snowing."

Florence Price's music has otherwise been nearly forgotten. Her published music is out of print, and only part of her unpublished work has been photocopied and placed in the Florence Price Collection at the University of Arkansas.

Like Amy Beach, Florence Price was considered to be out of date at the time of her death. She still composed as she had been taught in college, combining nineteenth-century harmony with traditional classical form. Yet Price's music is new and original in its own way. The rich musical heritage of African-Americans is found in much of our jazz, rock, and other forms of popular music; however, only Florence Price and a few other composers brought it to the symphony orchestras of America and all the world.

Vivian Fine
Courtesy of Vivian Fine

Seven
VIVIAN FINE
(1913-)

"**I** never *wanted* to be a composer," recalls Vivian Fine. "I *am* a composer, which is a different thing. It's not an intellectual decision, because economically it's a hard life. It's more of a calling. I think if you find yourself doing something that fascinates you and grips you, that's what you're going to do."

Vivian Fine was born on September 28, 1913, in Chicago. Her parents, David Fine and Rose Finder Fine, were Russian-Jewish immigrants who came to live in the United States when they were both young children. David was an intellectual, who spent much of his time reading, thinking, and discussing ideas. He supported his family by working at several different jobs, including hospital superintendent and office manager. Rose showed a talent for music and took a few piano lessons when she was twelve. She spent most of her adult life raising her and David's three daughters. Besides Vivian, they were Adelaide, born in 1910, and Eleanor, born in 1914.

Vivian showed an interest in music at a very young age. From age three or four, she especially liked her family visits to her mother's sister because she owned a piano. On one visit to Aunt Bertha's, five-year-old Vivian drew her hand lightly over the piano keys, and then threw herself down on the floor and began to kick and scream. Her parents were alarmed. Usually their middle daughter was a quiet, well-behaved child. In fact, this was the only temper tantrum Vivian would throw during her entire childhood.

"What's the matter, what's the matter?" Rose asked little Vivian, who had now begun to sob uncontrollably.

"I want to take piano lessons!" she replied.

The Fines didn't have any extra money to spend on piano lessons, but Rose felt that if Vivian wanted them this badly, she should have them. Aunt Bertha's piano was moved to the Fines' apartment. Rose gave Vivian her first lessons, but in just two months she had taught her everything she knew. Rose hired a neighborhood piano teacher, but after only two more months, she realized that that teacher didn't have any more to offer her daughter, either. Vivian had already worked her way through two teachers and she was still only five years old. However, Rose knew what step to take next.

She took Vivian to audition for a scholarship at the Chicago Musical College. Vivian won a scholarship and studied there for three years.

At age nine, Vivian took lessons from private teachers. She won another scholarship, this time to the American Conservatory, where she studied with Silvio Scionti. When Vivian was eleven, she was accepted as a student of a famous piano teacher in Chicago, Djane Lavoie-Herz. It seemed certain that Vivian was destined to become a great concert pianist, but her association with her new teacher lead her in quite a different direction.

Madame Herz had been a student of the Russian composer Alexander Scriabin. Scriabin had invented a unique system of composition connected with his mystical beliefs. Many of Madame Herz's students and friends were ardent admirers of Scriabin's music, and some shared his beliefs. "Scriabin was really a power," says Vivian Fine. He became a great influence on her work.

Madame Herz's piano studio was the gathering place for the musical avant-garde. Musicians and composers came there to perform new works and discuss methods of composition that were not yet accepted by the general public. Some composers who attended Madame Herz's musical soirees were Dane Rudhyar, Henry Cowell, and Herz's pupil Ruth Crawford Seeger.

At age thirteen, Vivian began to study music theory with Ruth. During one lesson, Ruth asked Vivian to compose a piece of music. Vivian went home and wrote her first composition. "It was a little different," she recalls, "not entirely conventional." When she returned for her next lesson, she played her composition for her teacher.

"I remember particularly the thoughtful look on Ruth's face when I turned around to look at her," says Fine. "And she said she liked my piece and asked me to write another one. That's how I started to write: because somebody asked me to write a piece." Vivian composed more and more works. "It became a passion for me to write," she says.

From the very beginning and throughout her career, Vivian Fine has composed in counterpoint or in a contrapuntal texture. ("Contrapuntal" is the adjective for "counterpoint." "Counterpoint" is also called "polyphony," meaning "many sounds.") Counterpoint or polyphony is music made up of two or more melodies played at the same time. Notes used to be called "points"; "counterpoint" means "point against point." In other words, the notes of one melody sound at the same time as the notes of one or more other melodies, automatically creating harmony. The more common way to compose music is to write one melody and then support it with chords, which supply the harmony. This is called homophony ("same sound").

Many composers have written in counterpoint, especially in the Baroque era. During the classical and Romantic eras that followed, most of the music written was homophonic. Many twentieth-century composers besides Vivian Fine returned to polyphony, while other composers used homophony, or a combination of the two textures. Almost all our popular and folk music is homophonic.

Vivian Fine attended one semester of high school, then dropped out of formal education. She felt she was learning things that didn't interest her. For instance, one teacher asked her to memorize how many post offices there were in the United States, and Vivian thought to herself, "I don't want to know that."

"My parents were very supportive of my not going to school," says Fine. "They understood about educating oneself all of one's life. There was a tradition in our household of constant reading. Whatever education I have is from extensive reading." Both of Vivian's parents were also self-educated, because their families couldn't afford to send them to school. At age eight, Vivian's father had to start working full time in a sweater factory, and at fourteen, her mother became a secretary, typing and taking shorthand.

After leaving school, Vivian didn't waste any of her time. She practiced the piano and had two piano lessons a week. She composed many hours a day and she continued to study composition with Ruth Crawford Seeger. "Ruth took me very seriously," says Fine. "When I got to be sixteen or seventeen, we really became friends."

Composers Dane Rudhyar and Henry Cowell were also interested in Fine's compositions. They looked at her work and talked to her or wrote letters to her, offering suggestions on how to improve it. At the age of sixteen, Fine wrote "Solo for Oboe," a composition Cowell especially admired. He arranged to have the piece performed at a concert in New York City sponsored by the Pan-American Association of Composers.

In 1931, at age eighteen, Vivian Fine moved to New York City, hoping to earn her living as a pianist while furthering her career as a composer. At first, she boarded with a family in Greenwich Village, and then she took her own "cold-water" apartment on East 54th Street. A friend told her there was an opening for a pianist at the Gluck-Sandor Dance Theater. Vivian auditioned and got the job.

At the time, great changes were taking place in the art of dance. Choreographers Martha Graham, Hanya Holm, Doris Humphrey, and Charles Weidman were developing a new style of dance, called modern dance, which was much different than traditional ballet. New music was needed to accompany the new kinds of body movements. By watching the modern dancers and playing piano for them, Fine learned what kind of music they needed. Her job as dance accompanist led to many opportunities to compose for dance.

Vivian Fine also began performing at concerts devoted to new music, an aspect of her career that lasted over sixty years. She played her own composition *Four Polyphonic Piano Pieces* on April 30, 1932, at the First Yaddo Festival of Contemporary American Music, in Saratoga Springs, New York.

Also during 1932, Fine became a regular member of the Young Composers' Group, founded by American composer Aaron Copland. Other members included Arthur Berger, Henry Brant, Bernard Herrmann, Irwin Heilner, and Elie Siegmeister. This informal club of young composers met every several weeks at Copland's studio to play and discuss their compositions. They also studied new music written by important contemporary composers, including Charles Ives, Anton Webern, and Darius Milhaud. Whenever a new composition was brought to a meeting, someone would exclaim, "Vivian, play it!" Fine was the best sight-reader in the group. She could give a fairly good performance of a piece while reading the notes for the first time.

Vivian Fine (far right) takes a bow after a performance of her composition Meeting for Equal Rights, 1866, *at Cooper Union, New York, April 23, 1976*
Courtesy of Vivian Fine

Aaron Copland was the informal leader of the group; however, he acted more like a referee. The members of the Young Composers' Group fought about almost everything except the name of their organization and the rule that members could be no older than twenty-five. Fine recalls, "There was not a lot of brotherly and sisterly love. We severely criticized each other's music." Bernard Herrmann always said, "It stinks," no matter what was played. Henry Brant wrote,

> *The best thing about our bunch is nobody likes anybody else's music—wouldn't touch it with a ten foot pole. Exceptions are me and Irwin—I like both his and my stuff and he says he thinks we're both terrible.*

Although some of the meetings of the Young Composers' Group were a little tense, Vivian benefited greatly from the experience. The group offered her moral support, connections in the musical world, and many helpful suggestions in her composing.

When Copland went to Mexico in November of 1932, he feared that the group would not hold together without him. He was right. The Young Composers' Group gave a concert of their works on January 15, 1933, and then disbanded.

In 1934, a friend of Vivian's introduced her to a sculptor named Benjamin Karp, who made portraits and animal sculptures out of wood and stone. Benjamin and Vivian hit it off and were married the following year. The *New York Daily Mirror* published photographs of the two creative artists and an article with the headline "We Won't Karp, We Think It's Fine." Over the years, Vivian has found it stimulating and helpful to be able to discuss artistic ideas with her husband, and she still does so today. Their marriage has now lasted more than fifty-six years.

In 1937, Doris Humphrey asked Vivian Fine to compose the music for a new dance she was choreographing. The dance was called *The Race of Life*, and was based on a new set of funny drawings with the same title by humorist James Thurber.

Thurber's six drawings, about the adventures of a middle-class American family, are entitled "The Start," "Spring Dance," "The Beautiful Stranger," "Night Creatures," "Indians," and "Finish Line." These scenes are all treated in a funny way. "The Beautiful Stranger" is not a shy, young girl, but a full-grown woman who has seen some hard times and knows how to survive them. The "Night Creatures" are weird and scary. To accompany them, Fine used an instrument called a Flexatone, which creates sliding, eerie sounds. The "Indians" were phony types, like the wooden statues that used to be found outside cigar stores. Fine wrote a comical parody of a popular song about Indians. She first wrote *The Race of Life* for piano; later, she arranged it for orchestra.

Other modern-dance choreographers wanted to use Vivian Fine's music. In the next two years, she composed *Opus 51* for Charles Weidman and *Tragic Exodus* and *They Too Are Exiles* for Hanya Holm.

At age twenty-five, Fine stopped working as a dance accompanist, but she continued to compose for dance.

Much later, in 1960, she composed *Alcestis*, which was choreographed by Martha Graham. In Greek mythology, Alcestis agreed to die in her husband's place and travel to Hades, the underworld. When the god Hercules heard about this, he went to Alcestis' grave and wrestled with Death so that she could come back to life.

While composing for dance, Fine was also writing other kinds of music. She studied composition privately with composer Roger Sessions for seven years, between 1935 and 1942. Sessions was one of the leading composition teachers in the United States between 1935 and 1980. Unlike many composer-instructors, Sessions did not encourage his students to compose in his style. He had many talented students who developed their own unique forms of expression. Milton Babbitt, for instance, went on to compose mostly electronic music, and Conlan Nancarrow began to write only for player piano. Sessions supplied Fine with direction, while giving her the freedom to develop her contrapuntal style.

Each of Vivian Fine's compositions is different from the others; however, her work can be divided into three periods. During the first of these, between 1926 and 1937, her music was harsh and stern, with many clashing sounds called dissonances. Henry Cowell wrote,

> *When I first met Vivian Fine she was a Chicago girl of seventeen, writing in the grimmest of dissonant styles. She had developed a technique for elimination of concord that gave her work an angular, unladylike manner. . . .*

Cowell was probably making a little joke when he used the adjective "unladylike." Dissonant, clashing tones create restlessness and tension in music, and are supposed to be masculine. Consonant, blending tones create stability and rest, and are considered to be feminine. Actually, assigning gender to consonance and dissonance is ridiculous. All music, written and enjoyed by both men and women, contains both consonance and dissonance. Most art music written in the twentieth century includes more dissonance than music of the previous centuries.

In Vivian Fine's second period of composition, between 1937 and 1944, her music became very consonant. In her third period, from 1945 to the present, Fine has combined elements of her first and second periods, creating more of a balance between consonance and dissonance.

In all her works, Fine has tried to write music that makes each musical instrument sound its best. To learn to do this, Fine attended many symphony concerts and listened carefully to how each instrument sounded. She showed her compositions to many musicians who played different instruments. They told her if her music was too difficult or awkward to play; and if it was, she would change it. Fine imagines the sounds of instruments while she is composing. "I have a certain instrument in mind while I'm writing," she says. "I can't write without that."

Like many other composers, Vivian Fine found it hard to make much money writing art music. Some composers of art music worried that if they charged a fee for the performance of their work, no one would want to play it. Others felt they had a right to make a living by composing.

The American Society of Composers, Authors, and Publishers (ASCAP) had already been established to collect money for the performances of popular music, but there was no organization to help serious composers collect fees and promote concerts of their music. This led to the founding of the American Composers Alliance (ACA).

Vivian Fine participated in the early stages of the American Composers Alliance. She hosted some of the planning sessions in her apartment. The first formal meeting of the ACA was held on December 19, 1937, at the Beethoven Association. A membership drive brought 184 composers into the ACA. Aaron Copland became the group's first president, serving from 1938 to 1944. The second president, Otto Luening, wrote, "We now became composer-business-men"—two careers that were often not suited for the same person. Vivian Fine later served as vice president of ACA, from 1961 to 1965.

Other organizations helped composers of art music get paid for their work and get their works known. In 1944, Broadcast Music, Inc. (BMI) paid ACA $10,000 for the right to perform its members' music over the radio. In 1954, Composers Recordings, Inc. (CRI) was founded to produce and sell recordings of art music. CRI has recorded much of Vivian Fine's music, including *Sinfonia and Fugato* for piano in 1952, *Alcestis* in 1960, and *Missa Brevis* in 1982. Fine has also played piano on a CRI recording. She accompanied violinist Ida Kavafian, performing Ruth Crawford Seeger's *Sonata for Violin and Piano* of 1926.

Benjamin Karp and Vivian Fine became parents in 1942, when their first daughter, Margaret (Peggy), was born. Their second daughter, Nina, was born six years later in 1948. As a busy young mother, Vivian composed less; however, she was always involved with music. She helped support her family by giving many private piano lessons. She also taught piano at New York University from 1945 to 1948 and at the Juilliard School in 1948. In 1949, Benjamin accepted a faculty position at State University of New York College at New Paltz, so the family moved to upstate New York.

Vivian Fine continued to teach piano privately until 1964. She taught composition classes at the State University of New York College at Potsdam in 1951 and at the Connecticut College School of Dance from 1963 to 1964. In 1964, she became a member of the music faculty at Bennington College in Vermont, where she taught composition until 1987. About her teaching career, Fine says, "I didn't have as much time as I would have liked to write, but I never felt resentful about the teaching. I enjoy teaching very, very much."

In 1956, Vivian Fine received her first commission, which was from the Rothschild Foundation. She had enjoyed using humor in *The Race of Life* and decided to use it again. The result was *A Guide to the Life Expectancy of a Rose,* for soprano and tenor voices, and flute, violin, clarinet, cello, and harp. Fine got the idea for the piece one Sunday while reading the gardening

Vivian Fine conducts a performance of her composition Teisko *for eight solo voices and string quartet (seated in the balcony), at Bennington College, May 22, 1976*
Courtesy of Vivian Fine

section of *The New York Times.* She clipped out an article, written by S. R. Tilley, and used it for her text. It begins:

> *How long a rosebush will grow and flower is seldom considered when it is planted in spring or fall. There are no tables of life expectancy and it is impossible to quote any real statistics as to the longevity of a rosebush.*

This is a very serious article for rose lovers, who take their rosebush-growing very seriously. S. R. Tilley certainly did not intend, even in his wildest dreams, to write lyrics for a musical composition. Fine makes the rosebush article funny not only by setting it to music, but also by the way she does it. She puts emphasis on unimportant syllables or words. For instance, the rather boring phrase "and it is possible" is stretched out to five beats when it would be more practical to get it over with in a quick two beats.

Another funny moment in the piece is after the sentence "At the Brooklyn Botanical Gardens there are many that have been flowering for 25 years." The flute and clarinet play a long, jumpy section, as if roses are busting out all over.

Fine composed other humorous pieces, including "Sea Turtle," for voice and piano, in 1971, and "Discourse of the Goatherds," for solo trombone, in 1989.

Fine has used a different combination of voices and instruments in nearly every piece she has written. In 1972, she composed *Missa Brevis*, for four cellos and taped voice. In preparation for the performance of this piece, recordings were made of soprano Jan DeGaetani singing four different voice parts, one by one. These four separate tracks were blended together on a single recording, so that it sounds as if four women are singing at the same time. In performance, this tape is accompanied by four live cellos.

Missa Brevis means "brief Mass." Fine creates her own version of the Mass, omitting some parts of it and adding other religious writings. She uses both Latin and Hebrew to remind us that the roots of Christianity are in the Jewish faith.

Vivian Fine has received many commissions, grants, and awards, including the Dollard Award in 1966 and a Ford Foundation grant in 1970. Nineteen eighty was a special year for Fine, during which she was awarded a Guggenheim fellowship, received a commission from the Martha Baird Rockefeller Foundation, and was elected a member of the American Academy and Institute of Arts and Letters.

In 1977, Fine's chamber opera, *The Women in the Garden,* was funded by a grant from the National Endowment for the Arts. Fine uses the word "chamber" to describe her opera because it is written for five voices and nine instruments, which could all fit in a good-sized room. Most operas include many more singers and a full orchestra, and are performed in a huge opera house. Many twentieth-century composers choose to write for fewer musicians because works that employ a great many musicians are so expensive to produce that they have little chance of being performed. *The Women in the Garden* is also shorter than most operas, lasting just over one hour instead of three or four. *The Women in the Garden* was premiered by the Port Costa Players in San Francisco on February 12, 1978.

The opera is centered around four famous women who meet in a garden: poet Emily Dickinson, modern dancer Isadora Duncan, and writers Gertrude Stein and Virginia Woolf. These historical characters sing words taken from their own writings. One tenor sings all the male roles, small parts that support the women characters. Sometimes the singers sing long solos and at other times they sing to each other in dialogue. The tempo, which doesn't change much throughout the piece, is a slow walking pace, the speed of relaxed conversation.

The Women in the Garden has no plot. Instead of telling a story, the opera gradually reveals the personalities of the women. Emily Dickinson sings her poem of faith, "The Sailor does not see the North, but knows the Needle can." Isadora Duncan sings a lament over her dead child. By the end of the opera, we feel as if we have known these women like close friends.

In 1984, with funding from a Koussevitsky Foundation grant, Vivian Fine composed *Poetic Fires* for piano and orchestra. She performed the piano part when the piece was premiered by the American Composers Orchestra, under the direction of Gunther Schuller, on February 21, 1985. When Fine was practicing *Poetic Fires*, she talked about being both composer and pianist for the same work.

> *I always compose away from the piano, and I never change a piece while I'm learning it. Once a work is finished, I forget about being a composer and approach it as a pianist.*

Vivian Fine has now been a composer for over sixty-five years. She has retired from teaching and the concert stage, but she continues to write music. She and Benjamin live in upstate New York, in a multilevel house with Benjamin's stone sculptures decorating the yard. Cows behind white picket fences are their closest neighbors. Both of their daughters followed in their footsteps—Peggy is a pianist and Nina is a singer and painter. Vivian's hobbies include reading and walking. Her main concern outside of music is world peace, which is reflected in her latest work, *Songs of Love and War* (1991).

One question Vivian Fine has been asked many times is: Is it harder for a woman to be a composer than a man? Fine answers, "Not for me, since my first composition teacher was a woman. Ruth Crawford [Seeger] wrote very bold music. With a tremendous example like that, I found it very natural to be a composer."

Fine has met with some prejudice, however. She recalls that in 1957, when her dance piece *Race of Life* was performed at the Juilliard School of Music, a male composer came up to her afterward and said, "That was nice orchestration. Did you do it yourself?"

"I'm certain he didn't intend to sound nasty," says Fine, "though it was a patronizing remark." As if a woman couldn't do a good job choosing which instrument would play which part of a composition!

When *The Women in the Garden* was premiered, the two male music reviewers from the San Francisco newspapers noisily left together after they had listened to only a small part of Fine's opera. One of the reviewers later explained that he knew within five minutes that he wasn't going to like the work, and could see how it would continue without actually having to sit through it. The other reviewer said it was "not an opera" since it lacked action and drama. Yet the large audience that listened to the entire piece offered Fine enthusiastic applause, and reviewer Charles Suttoni praised the work in *Musical America.*

In response to these incidents, Fine says: "I don't think that prejudices against women composers can be isolated from attitudes toward women in general. The women's movement has done a lot to eradicate negative attitudes, and that's being reflected in all professions. I think *now* is actually a good time to be a woman composer."

Joan Tower
Courtesy of G. Schirmer Music Publishers, Inc.

Eight
JOAN TOWER
(1938-)

◆

"The giant, majestic sequoia seems to me an incredible feat of balance," Joan Tower says about the oldest and biggest living thing in the world today. "Yet, in spite of its power and grandeur, its leaves are tiny, no larger than a thumbnail." The sequoia is what rose up in Tower's mind when she tried to describe her first composition for orchestra. Since its premiere in 1981, *Sequoia* has become one of the most popular and most frequently played orchestral works written within the last ten years.

Joan Peabody Tower was born on September 6, 1938, in New Rochelle, New York. Her father, George Warren Tower, belonged to a musical family, in which his mother was a pianist. George worked as a mining engineer, and he also sang and played the violin. Joan's mother, Anna Peabody Robinson, played the piano, like many young ladies of her generation; however, she was not a natural musician like her husband. Joan's sister, Ellen, was born nine years before her, in 1929, and her brother, George Jr., was born nine years after her, in 1947.

Joan spent the first nine years of her life in Larchmont, New York. She began taking piano lessons at age six, attended public elementary school, and enjoyed playing jacks and swapping picture-trading cards with her girlfriends. It seemed that her childhood would be much like those of thousands of other children growing up in the United States; however, after her ninth birthday, Joan's life changed dramatically. Her father accepted a position as a mine supervisor in the "land of tin"—Bolivia, South America. Joan was abruptly uprooted from her safe suburban neighborhood and catapulted up thirteen thousand feet in altitude to La Paz, nestled in the towering, snowcapped Andes Mountains.

At first Joan was overwhelmed by the exotic sights and sounds of her strange, new home. Everyone around her was yammering in not one but three foreign languages: Spanish, Aymara, and Quechua. The high, thin air rarely rose above a chilly fifty degrees. The Towers, who were a middle-income family in the United States, were considered to be very wealthy in Bolivia and moved into a big house with many servants. Big sister Ellen stayed in the United States to attend college, and little brother George was just a baby, so Joan felt that she had to face these many changes all alone.

Gradually, she adjusted to her new life. She learned to speak Spanish in just two months because she was anxious to communicate with her new school friends. She wandered into the kitchen and made friends with the Indian servants, Juan, Aida, and Mercedes. They taught Joan their language, Aymara. Although they wore only sandals on their feet, they protected their bodies from the cold with derby-shaped felt hats, woolen blouses, and heavy shawls. The women wore as many as six full skirts, one on top of another, of bright orange, red, pink, blue, green, and purple, but never two skirts of the same color next to each other.

Like most natives of South America, the Towers' servants practiced the Catholic religion. About every three days, Aida took Joan to festivals celebrating the feast days of saints. Throngs of people crowded into the streets to watch parades of large swaying statues, drummers, and flying banners. Some dressed in traditional costumes and danced ancient dances. Food, music, and fireworks added even more excitement to the celebrations.

On other days, Joan went with Aida to the marketplace. On display were not only fruits and vegetables but also blankets, pottery, llama-skin slippers, and other items that the native people had made by hand. Aida didn't pay the first price asked, but haggled with the vendor, just as all the shoppers did.

Joan's father frequently traveled to the many different

mines that he supervised. Sometimes his family stayed in La Paz, but other times they traveled with him on cargo planes with open holes for windows and by *auto carrel*—an automobile on railroad tracks. Some of the mines were in mountains seventeen thousand feet high, so far from railroads that teams of llamas had to carry the tin ore down the mountainsides.

Even taking piano lessons was an adventure in La Paz. Joan suspected that her piano teacher was really a witch. She had long black hair and she lived by herself, high up on a hill, in a big, creaking house that seemed haunted. The woman was the ex-wife of an old silent-movie star, and how she ended up alone in La Paz was a deep, dark mystery that Joan pondered. When Joan didn't practice enough, her teacher worked up such a rage that she seemed ready to fly around the room. She was very demanding of Joan because she was her most talented student.

Joan's happiest times in La Paz were after dinner, when the whole family gathered around the piano. Sometimes her father played the violin, but mostly he liked to sing songs from the twenties and thirties. Joan's mother accompanied him on the piano, while Joan improvised on South American percussion instruments, including maracas and castanets. Later in her life, when Joan composed music for orchestra, she would use many intricate rhythms and a great variety of percussion instruments in her works.

Joan loved horses and begged her father to buy her one. Horse racing in Bolivia was not the costly business it is in the United States. Mr. Tower was able to afford

Joan Tower, age fourteen, on her horse Aymara, in La Paz, Bolivia
Courtesy of Joan Tower

a second-class flat-racing horse, which Joan named Aymara, after the Aymara language. Aymara was so high-spirited that Joan had to be accompanied by his trainer whenever she rode him. Aymara won so many races that he was eventually moved up to the first-class category.

When Joan turned fourteen, her parents became concerned that she was running around La Paz too freely. Thinking she needed more discipline, they sent her to Santiago, Chile, to attend a strict private girls' high school called Santiago College. English was spoken there to accommodate the students, who were mostly wealthy foreigners. Joan had to wear an ugly green uniform with white cuffs, brown stockings, brown shoes, and a felt hat.

Joan spent most of her time at Santiago College breaking the rules. She started pillow fights in the halls. She sometimes managed to sneak off the school grounds without the necessary written permission. She and her friends liked to lounge around the pool of a swanky nearby hotel, posing as rich tourists.

Joan's father made sure that she had a piano teacher and a piano to practice everywhere she went, and Santiago College was no different. At one recital there, Joan played Chopin's very difficult "Revolutionary Etude." It gave her left hand lots to do and suited her rebellious spirit.

After completing her sophomore year at Santiago College, Joan rejoined her family, which had moved to Lima, Peru. The Towers planned to return to the United States in a few months. This was not enough time for Joan to enroll in another school, yet it was too much time to sit idle; so Joan and her father devised a unique curriculum for her. Mr. Tower requested that Joan attend a typing class because he thought typing was a useful skill; Joan asked to take horseback-riding lessons because she still loved to ride; and they both liked the idea of piano lessons.

When the Towers returned to the United States,

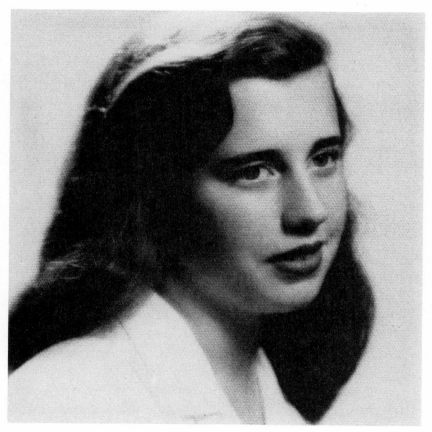

Joan Tower, age eighteen, at Walnut Hill High School
Courtesy of Joan Tower

Joan attended another boarding school, Walnut Hill, in Natick, Massachusetts, where she completed her last two years of high school. She took piano lessons from a fine teacher, Elizabeth Cobb, and accompanied the choir.

In 1957, Joan enrolled at Bennington College in Vermont. By then she was spending several hours a day practicing the piano, especially the music of her favorite composer, Beethoven. From very early on, Joan felt a strong connection to Beethoven, and still does today. Both composers are passionate, energetic, and rebellious—traits that are reflected in their music. Like Beethoven, Joan has an interest in complex rhythms and develops the same material in many different ways in one composition. Both composers prefer composing for musical instruments to composing for voice: Beethoven wrote only one opera, and Tower has not composed any vocal music.

Like many young women, Joan felt a mixture of many different emotions churning inside her. She was filled with a sense of longing and desire, which she didn't completely understand. She says now:

> *When you're young, you may feel lonely for one reason or another. You're not happy at home or you don't have a best friend. I got through a lot of this because of music. Music was like a haven for me. It made me feel worthwhile. Playing in recitals made me feel I was useful and important.*

Joan experienced one complicated feeling that was both thrilling and agonizing all at the same time. "I was boy-crazy, boooooy crazy!" Joan confesses. "But I was also very aggressive. I said what I wanted. I had a lot of energy. It takes a pretty strong guy to accept a strong woman. I'm sure I was too much for most of them."

At age nineteen, Joan began to take notice of a handsome young college professor who hung around the coffee shop on campus. She talked to him a few times and found him to be more sensitive than the boys her age. Soon she had a crush on him. She spent a lot of time daydreaming about him and finding out little things about him. One day she happily discovered that he liked music. Soon after, she got an opportunity to live out a scene she had fantasized many times.

One of Joan's music professors invited both her and her dreamboat professor to a party in his home. Joan took her place at the piano and gave an electrifying performance of the difficult Beethoven Sonata in A-flat Major, Opus 110, pouring forth all the passion she felt for this man who meant so much to her, sitting a mere four feet away.

Apparently he got the message. After Joan finished playing, everyone but her and the professor went into the kitchen. In a highly charged, emotional moment, he looked into her eyes and said, "Let's get out of here."

Joan wasn't quite sure what he had in mind, but she instantly knew what she really wanted. "Aw, no," she replied hastily, "I think we should go into the kitchen."

"I couldn't deal with my fantasy becoming a reality,"

Joan says now, years later. "That boy-crazy feeling was mixed up with a need for a lot of approval. When I found out what I could really do in music I better understood what it all meant."

One way Joan learned about her musical capabilities was by merely doing her homework. In one of her classes at Bennington, she was given an assignment to compose a piece. "I wrote this piece and I heard it," says Joan. "I don't remember the exact piece, but I remember how it felt. Hearing that piece was such a different musical experience than playing the piano."

Joan composed many more pieces. After she graduated from Bennington College in 1961, she enrolled as a graduate student in composition at Columbia University in New York City. To earn a living, Joan taught piano lessons, from 1962 to 1972, at the Greenwich Music School, a settlement house where people in the community could study music for reasonable fees.

Joan earned her master's degree in 1964 and her doctorate of musical arts in 1978, both at Columbia University. But after fourteen years of college, Joan still didn't think she was a mature composer. She hadn't yet discovered a style that was uniquely her own. She needed to compose more pieces.

Audiences, however, seem to want to hear, over and over, the same classical pieces, sometimes called old war-horses because they have survived for so long. Many performers are even reluctant to try out new works of music. But this didn't discourage Joan. She has always been willing to stick up for new music, no matter what anybody thought of it. She started the

Greenwich House Series of Contemporary Music Concerts and raised money to hire the best musicians to play the new music. Joan played piano at some of the concerts and wrote one piece per season for some of the players involved in the concerts. This gave her a chance to hear her compositions performed and to play many new works by other composers.

In 1969, Joan Tower formed her own musical chamber group, devoted to performing new works of music. The Da Capo Players consist of flute, clarinet, violin, cello, and piano. "Da capo" is an Italian musical term meaning "go back to the beginning" of a piece. The Da Capo Players often repeat a piece on the same program so that the audience can become more familiar

The Da Capo Players in 1980. From left to right: Joel Lester (violin), Patricia Spencer (flute), Andre Emelianoff (cello), Joan Tower (piano), and Laura Flax (clarinet)
Courtesy of Joan Tower

with a new work that they may not have an opportunity to hear again.

Except for a few changes, the same musicians have been part of the Da Capo Players for twenty-three years, a very long time for a musical group to hold together. The Da Capo Players have performed all over the United States and Canada, have made several recordings, and have won many awards, including the Naumburg Award for Chamber Music and a Fromm Music Foundation grant. They have premiered over a hundred new works of music and are now recognized as one of the finest chamber groups for new music in the United States.

Joan Tower wrote many pieces for the Da Capo Players to perform. To better understand how to compose for each individual instrument, she composed a solo piece for each of the other members in the group.

For flutist Patricia Spencer, Tower wrote *Hexachords* in 1972. This piece explores different speeds of vibrato. It also includes great contrasts between loud and soft sounds and between high and low registers of the flute.

In 1977, Tower composed a solo for violinist Joel Lester and dedicated it to the memory of her father. Tower's music is sometimes called "image-inspired," meaning that she thinks of an object and tries to describe it through music. Actually, the opposite is true. Tower composes a piece, which reminds her of an image, which she then uses as a title. Since her father was a mining engineer, Joan wanted to use the name of a metal in the title of her violin solo. She looked through his old geology textbooks and discovered that platinum was very malleable and could easily be stretched. While listening to her violin solo, Joan imagined a piece of platinum swirling higher and higher into the air and came up with the title *Platinum Spirals*.

The clarinet solo Tower wrote for Laura Flax in 1981 caused her to think of a falcon gliding gracefully across the sky. This popular piece, which she called *Wings*, is played by many great clarinetists in the United States.

When it was Andre Emelianoff's turn to have Tower write a piece for him, he insisted that it not be for cello alone. He wanted a whole orchestra to accompany him. So, in 1984, Tower wrote *Music for Cello and Orchestra*.

Tower also composed many pieces for the Da Capo Players to play as a group. These include *Breakfast Rhythms I and II* (1974–75), *Amazon* (1977), *Petroushskates* (1980), and *Noon Dance* (1982). In *Amazon*, Tower pays tribute to her childhood in South America. The motifs or ideas in *Amazon* lead into one another, much like the flowing waters of a mighty river. Tower later reworked *Amazon* so that a whole orchestra could play it. *Petroushskates* was inspired by *Petrouska*, a piece composed by Igor Stravinsky, one of Tower's greatest influences. After writing it, Tower imagined the smooth flow of skaters drawing figures on ice. She combined the title of the Stravinsky piece with "skates" to come up with *Petroushskates*—a carnival on ice.

By writing many pieces for the Da Capo Players, Joan learned to compose slowly, quietly, and patiently. She says:

> *It took a long time. I didn't consider myself a composer until very late, when I was in my thirties. I view Da Capo as my musical education because hearing my music on a regular basis became the best learning experience.*

In 1972, Joan began to teach composition part-time at Bard College in Annandale-on-Hudson, New York. Throughout the seventies, she spent half of the year traveling and performing with the Da Capo Players and the other half at home teaching and composing.

By 1981, Joan had become very successful in composing for solo instruments and small groups of instruments. She knew it was time to face up to the challenge of writing for full orchestra. When the American Composers Orchestra asked her to write a work, she accepted the invitation with both enthusiasm and trepidation. The result was *Sequoia*.

This work opens with a single, low G, which reminded Joan of the roots of a tree. Out of this single note grow harmonies, texture, rhythm, and tone colors, above and below it, carefully "balanced." Tower explains, "This 'balancing,' like the branching of a tree, continues to develop into more complex settings, as the 'branches' start to grow sub-branches." The music soars with energy, like the tip of a sequoia thrusting toward dizzying heights.

This single piece, whose premiere was enormously

successful, changed Joan Tower's life. She was launched into the dazzling orchestral world, which was much more visible and glamorous than the modest chamber-concert circuit she had known. Joan found herself sitting in the famous Avery Fisher Hall listening to her own music being played by the New York Philharmonic conducted by Zubin Mehta in a televised United Nations concert. Later Leonard Slatkin and the St. Louis Symphony took *Sequoia* all around the world, performing it in London and Tokyo. Over thirty orchestras in the world have performed *Sequoia* and many more program it each new season. Joan appeared as guest composer with many orchestras and gave many pre-concert lectures. Thousands of people applauded her music and many newspapers wrote articles about her. Suddenly she was more famous than she had ever dreamed she would be.

After all this excitement, Joan felt she no longer had time to perform in the Da Capo Players. The decision was hard—the Players had been a big part of her life for fifteen years—but she wanted to concentrate on composing.

Joan had been active in an organization called Meet the Composer since its beginning in 1974. The purpose of Meet the Composer was to help the American public become more aware of composers living and working today. In 1985, Leonard Slatkin invited Joan Tower to become a Meet the Composer composer-in-residence for the St. Louis Symphony.

What is it like to be a composer who "lives with" an orchestra? Joan answers,

Joan Tower with conductor Leonard Slatkin, 1987
Courtesy of Joan Tower

> *At first it was scary to me, coming from a chamber group of*
> *five players. A major orchestra has a large bureaucracy, staff,*
> *conductor, and over 100 musicians. At first, I didn't know how*
> *to deal with all this, and the [orchestra] people were not certain*
> *how to deal with me.*

Joan attended many rehearsals and performances of
the St. Louis Symphony. She got to know the musicians personally and professionally. She appeared on
panels and at lectures, discussing new music. Whenever she spoke she liked to introduce herself by saying,
"I'm alive and I'm a woman." These two facts are so

obvious that the audience usually laughed, yet Joan mentioned them for a serious reason. She says,

> Not too many orchestra audiences hear music by live composers and very few hear music by a woman. I'm just reminding them of this, and they think, "Oh, yeah, there hasn't been any woman composer here in the last ten years, now that you mention it." I think this is changing, but we [women composers] have a long way to go.

As part of her job as composer-in-residence, Joan viewed scores and listened to tapes of over three hundred new pieces a year, submitted by other composers who hoped to have their works performed by the St. Louis Symphony. Before the Meet the Composer Orchestra Residency Program, no one was available to consider all the new music coming into orchestras. "[The new compositions] got shoved into a closet or sent back to the composers without anyone looking at them," says Joan. To be fair in her selection process, Joan removed the names of the composers from the works before she judged them. She wanted to give unknown composers just as much of a chance as famous composers. "I discovered some composers I had never heard of through this system," she says. Joan then passed the best pieces on to Leonard Slatkin, who made the final decision.

Joan Tower also organized a series of chamber music concerts much like the one she started years earlier at the Greenwich House. She called on musicians in the orchestra to play in the concerts, and she made all the decisions on what music would be programmed. Joan says, "I was a little biased toward women because my [male] colleagues are not terribly good at finding women composers. I brought a lot of women out to St. Louis." Joan commissioned works by Joan LaBarbara, Marilyn Shrude, and Margaret Dewys. She also programmed pieces by Kathryn Alexander, Nancy Chance, Sofia Gubaidulina, Libby Larsen, Tania Leon, Elizabeth Maconchy, and Joyce McKeel.

Of course, Joan Tower's most important job as composer-in-residence was to compose. In her three years of residency, she composed two works for the St. Louis Symphony, *Island Rhythms* (1985) and *Silver Ladders* (1986).

In *Silver Ladders*, many different melodies or scales move upward at different speeds, climbing musical ladders. Some of the lines move slowly and dreamily; others ascend quickly. In contrast to this feeling of climbing, Tower includes solos for clarinet, oboe, marimba, and trumpet. The *"Silver"* in the title reflects both the solid and the molten states of that metal. Silver can take the form of bold, heavy blocks as well as shimmering, liquid streams.

In April 1990, *Silver Ladders* competed against 140 other new orchestral works to win the $150,000 Charles B. Grawemeyer Award, the largest cash prize awarded in music. The judging for the Grawemeyer includes three panels, the last of which is a group of listeners who are not musicians. Joan recalls,

When I received the award I felt honored to be chosen by the third panel because a professional has a certain way of listening

to music which is more sophisticated on a certain level, and a nonprofessional just listens to the music. That's the kind of person I'm trying to reach.

Tower's other works include a piano concerto, *Homage to Beethoven* (1986), and three *Fanfares for the Uncommon Woman* (1986), a tribute to Aaron Copland's *Fanfare for the Common Man.* The third fanfare, which premiered at Carnegie Hall on May 5, 1991, was performed by two brass quintets, members of the New York Philharmonic and the Empire Brass and was conducted by Zubin Mehta. This performance was

Joan Tower with conductor Zubin Mehta, 1981. Photograph by Kathleen M. Hat
Courtesy of Joan Tower

televised by PBS for international distribution. Joan's newest orchestral work, *Concerto for Orchestra*, was commissioned by the New York Philharmonic, Chicago Symphony, and St. Louis Symphony, and premiered in St. Louis on May 16, 1991.

Joan Tower thinks her best pieces are her most popular ones. She says,

> I think of my pieces as being my children because I have no children. I have some stars and I have some delinquents. Some of them take off and others just kind of mope around. I think of all my pieces as being horrible when they first go out. It takes about sixty thousand people to tell me that they're O.K.

In April 1991, Tower and several other American composers were chosen to represent American music in the Soviet Union. *Silver Ladders*, *Island Prelude*, *Wings*, and *Petroushskates* were all performed in Moscow. "It's fascinating to hear orchestras from other countries play my music," says Joan. "They have a different kind of energy."

Since 1988, Joan Tower has held the Asher Edelman Chair at Bard College, a teaching position that allows her time to compose. "I love to see certain students get hooked on music and turn their lives around," says Joan. Recently three of her students had pieces performed by the Hudson Valley Philharmonic.

Joan teaches two days a week and composes on the other five. "I find it hard to take a day off," she admits. On her composing days, she works three hours in the morning, takes an hour and a half off for lunch, then writes for another four hours in the afternoon.

Joan has little time for anything else. She does enjoy tennis, though, and traveling with her music. She spent 1991 learning to play the viola. She lives with her male companion of seventeen years, a retired businessman and amateur pianist who recently took up the cello.

Does Joan Tower have any advice to young people who want to be composers? "Yeah. Form your own group and play in it. Then by playing you'll find a natural way of composing."

This method has certainly worked for her.

Ellen Taaffe Zwilich. Photography by Cori Wells Braun
Courtesy of Ellen Taaffe Zwilich

Nine
ELLEN TAAFFE ZWILICH
(1939-)

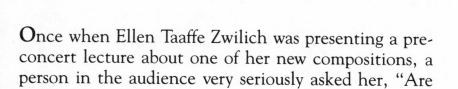

Once when Ellen Taaffe Zwilich was presenting a pre-
concert lecture about one of her new compositions, a
person in the audience very seriously asked her, "Are
you a *living* composer?"

The question sounds absolutely ridiculous, and yet it
didn't surprise Zwilich all that much. "I think that
most people are under the impression that all music
has already been written by dead people," she says,
with a faint Southern drawl.

Make that *European* dead people. "American composers are shadow figures and the general public is
almost completely unaware of us," comments Zwilich.
As for women composers, Zwilich says that "One

hundred years [ago] . . . society simply didn't recognize female achievements." Women composers have had to struggle to change the views of the public.

Born on April 30, 1939, Ellen became the adopted daughter of Edward and Ruth Taaffe. The Taaffes lived in Miami, Florida, where Edward was an airline pilot and Ruth worked as a homemaker. As a toddler, Ellen's favorite plaything was a toy xylophone. When she was a little older, she began to explore the Taaffes' piano, which no one in the family played. By age five, she was making up little piano pieces and songs.

Later that same year, Ellen began lessons with a neighborhood piano teacher. Ellen was disappointed by the boring little pieces the teacher assigned her. She felt that her own compositions sounded much better, but she didn't even think to play them for her teacher. She knew that the teacher wouldn't approve of her playing anything that was not in her piano lesson book, and might even forbid her to do it.

At age ten, Ellen began writing down her compositions. Soon after, she took up violin and trumpet, and played in the school orchestra and band. Although music absorbed much of her time, Ellen loved to play outdoors in the warm Miami sunshine. She especially enjoyed water sports—swimming, boating, and water-skiing. The Taaffe family did a lot of traveling. During one trip to New York, their plane landed in a dramatic blizzard. Ellen pressed her nose against the glass and caught her breath. The white swirling snowstorm was a thrilling contrast to the sandy beaches and palm trees of her home.

In high school, Ellen held the prestigious position of concertmistress, given to the best violinist in the orchestra. She was also first trumpet in the band. She tried her hand at conducting, and, of course, she continued to compose. She wrote a school fight song, which her classmates sang at football and basketball games. By age eighteen, she was composing pieces for orchestra.

After graduating from high school in 1956, Ellen majored in composition at Florida State University in Tallahassee, where she had many different musical experiences. Her musician friends played all her compositions as fast as she could write them, an opportunity not all young composers are fortunate enough to have. Ellen also sang in the Collegium Musicum, a singing group that performed music written in the Middle Ages and Renaissance. She played violin in an orchestra that performed for conducting classes given by Hungarian composer Ernst von Dohnányi.

Ellen did not limit herself to serious music from a classical tradition. She also played the trumpet in the university's jazz band. The music she composes now sounds nothing like jazz; however, she says that playing jazz influenced the way she thinks as a composer. "It's not something that's easily described," she says, "but it's an approach to rhythm, certain kinds of melodic development, and improvisation."

Ellen received her bachelor of music degree in 1960 and her master of music degree two years later. She was then ready to begin her career as a professional musician. Her first job was a teaching position at Converse College in Spartanburg, South Carolina.

After one year, Ellen discovered that being tucked away in a quiet little town was not the life for her. New York City was the musical center of the United States, and that was where she wanted to go. "I came to New York to study and to grow and develop," she says. "I wasn't entirely sure at that point where it would lead me."

Striking out alone in the big city is a precarious adventure for a young woman. "Looking back on it now," says Zwilich, "it seems rather chancy and difficult, but I was very excited about it. Many of the things that are important to do are a little bit scary or challenging or difficult, but it's great fun, too. I had a wonderful time coming to New York."

By then, Ellen had chosen the violin over the piano and trumpet as her major instrument; however, she wasn't happy with the sound she produced. She says, "I had gotten to the point where I was either going to play the violin much better or I was going to break it over my knee."

Ellen began studying violin with Ivan Galamian, who also taught two famous violinists, Itzhak Perlman and Pinchas Zukerman. She joined the ranks of the many violinists in New York who were trying to earn their living as free-lance performers. For one concert season, Ellen worked as an usher at Carnegie Hall, where she heard many great performers on the job, without the expense of tickets. She also taught music theory at Mannes College of Music and Hunter High

School. During her second year in New York, Ellen auditioned for the American Symphony Orchestra and was awarded a position in the violin section, which she held for seven years.

In August of 1967, a friend arranged a blind date between Ellen and another violinist, Joseph Zwilich. He was born in Hungary and had emigrated to the United States at a young age. He studied violin with Oscar Shumasky and had worked as a professional musician for many years. On the evening of their date, when Ellen opened her door for Joseph, they both burst out laughing. Their date wasn't so "blind" after all. Ellen had known Joseph previously; she just didn't put his name and face together until that moment.

Joseph and Ellen attended the Metropolitan Opera's production of Amilcare Ponchielli's *La Gioconda*; however, they didn't sit together. Joseph took his place in the orchestra pit—he actually had to work that night—while Ellen sat in the audience. Afterward, they dined at a Hungarian restaurant. Two years later, on June 22, 1969, Joseph and Ellen were married. After the ceremony, they celebrated with a small group of friends at the same Hungarian restaurant.

In 1970, Ellen began working on her doctorate of musical arts in composition at the Juilliard School of Music. There she studied with two American composers, Elliott Carter and Roger Sessions. About them, she says,

> *My teachers were immensely helpful in my development. They allowed me my independence, the best thing you can say about*

a teacher. Composition can't really be taught, it is a lifelong learning. . . . As a composition student I learned from observing the ways in which my teachers worked. Seeing how they thought about what they were doing helped me to clarify my thinking about my own work.

By 1971, Ellen felt that her long apprenticeship was over. The many, many compositions she had written before then had just been for practice. She had arrived at a point in her development where she was producing professional works. "This is really the best that I can do," she thought, then. "This is me." In 1975, Ellen Taaffe Zwilich became the first woman to graduate with a doctorate in composition from Juilliard.

With her violin playing, teaching, and composing, Ellen began to feel like a juggler. It became increasingly difficult to keep all the balls in the air all at once. Teaching was very demanding and took the same kind of energy as composing. Playing other composers' music distracted her from her own music, which was constantly taking shape in her thoughts. Ellen decided to plunge into a new life, to become totally immersed in her composing. This was a frightening decision. She knew it would be extremely difficult to earn a living as a composer; yet there was a greater risk than that involved. She was putting all her hopes and dreams on the line. She says,

I really wanted to focus on composing, but I had never actually done it. A lot of people think that they would love to spend all their life painting or writing and when the opportunity arises,

they find out it's not right for them. It takes a certain tempera-
ment in order to be a self-starter.

As a full-time composer, Ellen would have no boss
telling her what kind of works to compose, when to
start them, and how many hours a day she should
spend on them. But she had a lot of confidence in
herself and believed she was doing the right thing.

> *No matter what your track record, when you try to do something*
> *you've never done before, you risk falling on your face. So you*
> *have to work up courage. But I have this drive; it's sometimes*
> *an uncomfortable feeling, almost like an itch, but in some ways*
> *it's been my best friend, keeping me going.*

During the seventies, Zwilich composed several important works. In 1973, she wrote *Symposium,* a work
for orchestra, which was premiered by the Juilliard
Orchestra under the direction of composer and conductor Pierre Boulez.

Also in 1973, Joseph planned a recital tour of Europe. Ellen composed Sonata in Three Movements for
Violin for her husband so that he would have a composition of hers to play in his European recitals. In
composing the piece, Ellen thought about what kind
of music sounds best on violin. She also thought about
the particular way Joseph played the instrument. Ellen
wrote:

> *The composition grew out of my feelings for Joseph as well as*
> *from my particular fondness for the violin. . . . I wrote this for*
> *him, felt it was his piece. I loved his sense of timing, of*

proportion, the way he could shape a melodic line. . . . [And] I
wanted to use the things I most love about the violin—the kind
of sonorities you can get out of this wonderful instrument of
wood.

The following year, Zwilich composed String Quartet, 1974. It was performed at the 1976 World Music
Days in Boston. Richard Pittman, the musical director
of the Boston Musica Viva, heard the work and was
very impressed with it. In 1979, he asked Zwilich to
compose a work for this orchestra.

Ellen was very excited about receiving this commission. She set to work on what would become the
Chamber Symphony, for flute, piccolo, clarinet, bass
clarinet, violin, viola, cello, and piano. Ellen wanted
to try to create a piece that would make these few
instruments sound like a full orchestra.

Tragedy struck while Ellen was busy with her *Chamber Symphony*. Joseph was viewing a performance of the
Stuttgart Ballet at the Metropolitan Opera House when
he suffered a massive heart attack. He died in the same
auditorium where he had worked as a member of the
Metropolitan Opera Orchestra for so many years.

When Ellen felt ready to return to her work on the
Chamber Symphony after Joseph's death, she found that
the way she felt about it had completely changed. It
turned out to be a much different piece from the one
she had planned. About this, she says:

It's still very difficult for me to listen to the Chamber
Symphony. *. . . I loved Joe very dearly, and miss him to this*
day, yet his death taught me nothing so much as the joy of being

alive—the joy of breathing, walking, feeling well, swimming, the joy of being human. Suddenly all talk of method and style seemed trivial; I became interested in meaning. I wanted to say something, musically, about life and living.

Ellen dedicated the *Chamber Symphony* to the memory of Joseph. The work was eventually performed all over the world. It was televised in Sofia, Bulgaria, and aired by the British Broadcasting Company.

Ellen Taaffe Zwilich was awarded a Guggenheim fellowship, which allowed her to work on her Symphony No. 1 (Three Movements for Orchestra). For this work, she became the first woman composer to be awarded the Pulitzer Prize in Music. She had won many other awards and prizes before; however, this one was different. The Pulitzer is awarded each year to the best work in each of several fields—fiction, poetry, drama, history, and so on. Many awards are given for various kinds of journalism. For this reason, newspapers give lots of publicity to Pulitzer Prize winners, making the public very aware of them. Suddenly, Ellen Taaffe Zwilich was famous outside of the musical world. Many orchestras and musicians wanted her to compose pieces for them. She was offered more commissions than she could handle all at once. Zwilich recalls one request that she almost turned down.

There's a funny story behind my string trio. Somebody I hadn't seen in quite a while called me, and asked me if I would be interested in doing a work for their first concert. I said that I didn't have the time, but we kept talking for a while, and during the conversation I started to hear music. The trio was already

beginning to take shape in my head. So I said I'd think it over,
and I did, throughout the rest of the day, and, I guess, through
the night as well. In any event, I woke up the next morning,
and the whole opening section was waiting to be written down.

In February 1984, Zwilich flew to San Francisco to discuss the composing of a symphony, commissioned for the San Francisco Symphony by Dr. and Mrs. Ralph I. Dorfman. While attending a rehearsal of the orchestra, Zwilich was struck by the strong, warm tone of its cello section. The cellos inspired her to compose a symphony with ideas taken from the concerto form. But instead of having the orchestra accompany a solo cello, Zwilich decided to treat the *whole* cello section as a single instrument. Her Symphony No. 2 became her *Cello Symphony.*

The New York Philharmonic commissioned Zwilich to compose *Symbolon* in 1988. Zwilich traveled on a world tour with the orchestra, introducing her work to audiences in London, Amsterdam, Berlin, Paris, Hong Kong, Tokyo, and other cities. *Symbolon* was first performed in Leningrad (now St. Petersburg), making it the first American orchestral piece to be premiered in the Soviet Union.

At this time, Russia and the United States were still engaged in a cold war and arms race. However, Russian and American musicians got along just fine. They shared the same interest in creating and performing new music. The Russian public was overjoyed to hear a new symphonic work by an American composer. People who could barely afford food and clothes bought concert tickets. Ellen was overwhelmed by the response of the Russian people to her music. Many people came on stage to offer her flowers and other small presents. She had given them a piece of music to listen to and, in return, they wanted to give something to her.

Zwilich has written many other pieces on commission, including *Celebration* (1984) for the Indianapolis Symphony Orchestra; Double Quartet for Strings (1984) for the Chamber Music Society of Lincoln Center; Concerto for Trumpet and Five Players (1984) for the Pittsburgh New Music Ensemble; Concerto for Piano and Orchestra (1986) for the American Symphony Orchestra and Detroit Symphony Orchestra; *Tanzspiel* (1987) for the New York City Ballet; and Concerto for Trombone (1989) commissioned by the Chicago Symphony Orchestra. In the nineties she plans to compose an oboe concerto for John Mack and the Cleveland Orchestra and a Third Symphony for the New York Philharmonic. This makes Ellen Taaffe Zwilich one of the few composers today who supports herself entirely on commissions, prizes, performances, and royalties.

Ellen Taaffe Zwilich lives alone in a modern one-bedroom high-rise apartment in the Bronx, which is a convenient fifteen-minute drive from Lincoln Center. Her living room is decorated with a collection of paintings, and her desk overlooks the Hudson River. Part of her home is a comfortable place to relax and the other part is a cluttered workspace.

Zwilich starts most every day by composing for several hours. Before beginning a new work, she sketches many ideas over a long period of time. She develops her ideas by improvising on the piano and violin and notating her musical ideas. About her method of working, she says,

Music's been running through my subconsicous all night, so when I get up, I turn off the phone and become unavailable. . . . I do a lot of thinking before I begin a new work. But then, once I'm writing, something mysterious happens. Something beyond explanation—not so much as escape from reality as a confrontation with a deeper reality. You've got to be prepared, once you're well into a new work, to let it take you somewhere you've never been before.

I spend a few hours a day actively engaged in writing music, but being a composer is like being a writer of any sort—there's never a moment you're not working. I attend concerts as a composer, think about life as a composer.

Ellen Taaffe Zwilich is the subject of this Peanuts *comic strip, published October 13, 1990*
Used by permission of United Media

Ellen Taaffe Zwilich sums up her life's work by stating:

*It seems to me that there is something very deep about music;
[it's] in the same category as falling in love or a religious
experience. People do things they feel to be deeply enriching,
because they are totally pulled along, because they want to. . . .
I can't imagine life without music at the center of it.*

Laurie Anderson. Photograph by Robert Mapplethorpe © *1988*
Used by permission of the Robert Mapplethorpe Foundation

Ten
LAURIE ANDERSON
(1947–)

Laurie Anderson has created something called a drum suit. She took apart an electronic drum machine and wired its various parts into a jumpsuit. She puts on the jumpsuit and plays her body like a musical instrument. She strikes her fist against her rib cage and it booms like a bass drum. She thumps her collarbone and it emits the sound of a tom-tom. A knee slap *shabooms* like a whack on a high-hat cymbal.

Laurie Anderson holds a master's degree in sculpture, and you might call her drum suit a sculpture. However, this work of art is not complete until she slips it on and goes into action. Her drum suit is actually "performance art."

In the early seventies the term "performance artist" was invented for people like Laurie Anderson who didn't fit into any one category. Anderson works as a composer, sculptor, performer, photographer, film-maker, vocalist, violinist, writer, set designer, and electronic engineer all at once. "The best thing about the term 'performance art,' " says Laurie, "is that it includes just about everything you might want to do."

Laurie Anderson was born on June 5, 1947, in Glen Ellyn, a suburb of Chicago. Her father, Arthur, worked for a Chicago paint dealer. At age thirty-two, he eloped with the boss's daughter, Mary, who was seventeen. Arthur and Mary Anderson had eight children—four boys and four girls—of whom Laurie was second in line. Eventually Mary's father forgave Arthur for running off with his teenaged daughter. Arthur became successful enough in the paint business to support his large family comfortably while Mary stayed home to care for the children.

Laurie began taking violin lessons when she was five, and she progressed very rapidly. Her parents encouraged music in their home and the Anderson children formed a family band. But growing up in such a large, noisy family was hard for Laurie. She wished she had more time to herself to just sit around and think about things.

At age eight, Laurie was given the job of taking care of her twin baby brothers. She liked having the responsibility and grew very close to them. One day, while out for a walk, she took them by a shortcut across a frozen lake, and the ice broke. The heavy strollers plunged into the icy water, and Laurie jumped in after them. She felt guilty about nearly drowning her brothers, but she was also proud that she was able to save them.

Three years later, Laurie heard a minister on a religious radio show predict the end of the world. She spent a whole year reading the Bible and trying to warn people about Doomsday. Toward the end of that year, Laurie began writing down her thoughts in a journal. She noted that many things in life—such as the end of the world—were unpredictable.

Laurie continued to study the violin and practiced very hard. She auditioned and was accepted into the Chicago Youth Symphony. By the time she entered high school, it seemed likely that she would pursue a career as a concert violinist. But then one day, at age sixteen, Laurie quit the violin cold turkey.

She realized that, if she became a concert violinist, that would be *all* she would be able to do in life. She would have to spend hours and hours a day trying to sound as good as all the stiff competition. This was too narrow a form of self-expression for her. Laurie wanted to try to use music and art differently from other performers. She says, "Giving up practicing was one of the few things in my life that I am truly proud of."

After graduating from high school in 1965, Laurie was eager to get out of Glen Ellyn and strike out on her own. She moved to New York and enrolled in Barnard College as an art history major. It was hard to find a good, inexpensive place to live in the crowded city. Laurie stayed in a "hotel for desperate single secretaries" and, later, in an abandoned loft.

Laurie Anderson completed a bachelor's degree in art in 1969. Right after graduation, she needed some fast cash. She designed *The Package*, a mystery story in drawings. She looked in the phone book and decided that Bobbs-Merrill Publishing Company was her best bet because it was only one bus fare away. However, when she arrived at the publisher's offices, the receptionist told her that no one had time to see her. Laurie replied, "Do you mind if I just wait here a while?" She sat in the lobby, staring straight ahead, for five hours, until an editor who had been dashing in and out of her office exclaimed, "I can't stand seeing you sitting there. What do you want?"

Laurie showed the editor her drawings; the editor called in a business person; and they all signed a contract on the spot. Laurie recalls, "It was satisfying to think that maybe the rules weren't quite as strict as I had thought, that you could just try something."

This experience encouraged her to return to school to study sculpture. She claims that she was dismissed twice for working with material that wasn't "permanent enough"; however, in 1972, she managed to complete her master's degree.

One material that isn't very "permanent" is the honking of car horns, the main element in her piece "Automotive," created in 1972. For this work, Anderson composed a color-coded "symphony" score. She assembled an "orchestra" of cars, trucks, and motorcycles around a bandshell in Rochester, Vermont, and directed the drivers of the vehicles to honk their horns at various times.

Some of Laurie Anderson's "sculptures" are more like inventions. The concept behind her "Handphone Table" is that we can hear through our bones. Anderson installed a tape recorder in a pine table, then insulated it with seventeen alternating layers of rubber and lead. On the tabletop, she cut two circular depressions and lined them with metal. You can hear music played on the hidden tape recorder only if you place your elbows in the depressions and hold your head in your hands. Your arm bones conduct the vibrations of sound from the elbow rests to your ears.

From 1970 to 1974, Laurie Anderson lived with other artists in the downtown section of New York nicknamed SoHo because it is *South* of *Ho*uston Street. Painters, sculptors, dancers, composers, poets, and actors worked side by side, sometimes creating works in several media at once. Although SoHo was in the big city, it had a small-town atmosphere: Everybody knew everybody else.

Laurie got to know some of the artists even better by writing articles about them for *Artforum, ARTnews,* and other magazines. She liked having the opportunity to go over to an artist's home and "kind of spook around, see what was in his refrigerator."

SoHo was also the home of Steve Reich and Philip Glass, two important composers in the development of minimalist music. Minimalist music consists of short melodies repeated many times, with few chord changes, and a strong, steady beat. Laurie Anderson was greatly influenced by the work of her neighbors Reich and Glass. Many of her own compositions are in the minimalist style.

Although Laurie studied art in college, she didn't forget her many years of formal musical education during her youth. She also stuck with her early choice of musical instrument: the violin. "I like hand-held instruments," she says. "There is also something desperate-sounding about a violin that I can identify with."

Much of Anderson's work with the violin has been finding different ways to alter it. To create her "cassette violin," she hid a speaker inside a violin body so the violin could play a tape of her playing the violin.

Laurie used her "cassette violin," along with a pair of ice skates and two blocks of ice, in her performance-art piece called *Duets on Ice*. During 1974 and 1975, she presented this piece on various street corners in New York City and in Genoa, Italy. She put on the skates, embedded the blades in the blocks of ice, then improvised on the violin, playing a duet with her prerecorded self. Occasionally she stopped the music to chat with the gathering audience. Laurie says, "I talked about the parallels between skating and violin playing—blades over a surface—and about balancing, and what it means to play a duet with yourself—it's like coordinating your skates—trying to keep time." When the ice melted and Laurie's skates hit pavement, the piece ended.

A violin and pair of ice skates are very common objects; however, when Anderson combines them in

Duets on Ice, she gives us a chance to look at them in a completely new way. The familiar is transformed into something strange.

In 1976, Laurie Anderson created the "viophonograph" for her piece *For Instants*. She removed the strings of a violin, fitted a turntable on it, and installed a phonograph needle in the middle of the bow. On the turntable she placed a 45 r.p.m. record cut with one long note per band.

Her most famous invention and the one she uses the most in performance is her "tape-bow violin." She removed the strings from a violin and installed a tape-playback head on the bridge. She removed the horse-hair from the bow and threaded it with a length of magnetic tape on which there is a short prerecorded message. If she runs the bow slowly across the violin, the voice on the tape is deep and distorted. If she runs the bow more quickly, the tape sounds more like a regular speaking voice. If the bow is run backward, the message is played backward. "No" on the up-bow becomes "one" on the down-bow. "Yes" becomes "Say."

Laurie often plays a portion of the message several times before revealing all of it. The audience hears: "Ethics is the aesthetics of the few . . . the few . . . the few." The whole sentence is actually a quote from Lenin, founder of the Communist party in Russia: "Ethics is the aesthetics of the future."

Anderson has written a piece for "tape-bow" quartet. She converted the traditional instruments of a string quartet—two violins, viola, and cello—into "tape-bow" instruments, equipped with recordings of dogs barking. The people in the audience *see* a string quartet playing; they *hear* dogs barking. It's funny, and yet there's a serious side to it, too. Things in life are sometimes not what they seem to be.

Some of Laurie Anderson's pieces sound so wacky you might think she has discovered an entirely new mode of self-expression all her own. Anderson's methods, however, have roots in both the Dada movement in art and the "chance music" of American composer John Cage.

The Dada movement was a reaction against traditional values in society. It was founded after World War I in Zurich, Switzerland, by painter Marcel Duchamp and sculptor Jean Arp. *Dada* is the word French children use for "hobbyhorse." A typical Dada painting is a copy of Leonardo da Vinci's famous portrait the "Mona Lisa" decorated with a mustache.

In 1951, John Cage wrote *Imaginary Landscapes, No. 4* for six performers and twelve radios. The score gives precise instructions to the performers about how and when to turn the tuning and volume dials on the radios. In another Cage piece, *4'33"* (1952), the composer instructs a performer to *not* make a sound for 4 minutes and 33 seconds.

Laurie Anderson is also a little quirky about the way she lives her life. She claims that she spent the whole year of 1973 in bed:

> *My rule was that I wouldn't get up until I wanted to get up. And I would stay there until I could think of something that I wanted to do, not something that I had to do.*

It was quite an exercise. I didn't read and I didn't listen to music. I just looked out the window and thought about what I had done before and about what I could do.

Laurie did get up in the evenings to go teach Egyptian architecture and Assyrian sculpture at City College of the City University of New York. She enjoyed sitting in a dark room, showing slides of artwork, and talking about them to her students. This setting, however, put her in a dreamy mood. She forgot the facts and made up stories about the pharaohs and their adventures. When final exams came up, Laurie had a hard time deciding what to put on the test because she couldn't remember exact details of the stories she had told her students. She decided to quit her job before she got fired.

After that, Laurie continued to tell stories in the dark, but not as a teacher. She would be onstage and the people would be in the audience. That idea excited her so much she got out of bed and got right to work on it. But in the summer of 1975 it got too sweltering hot in New York to do anything.

Laurie remembered watching cartoon characters who would hang signs on their doorknobs that read: GONE TO THE NORTH POLE. She figured, Why not? She spent a few weeks researching how to survive out in the open in a very cold climate, then bought camping equipment and other supplies that she would need.

When she was all ready to go, she stood on Houston Street in New York City and stuck out her thumb. Laurie hitchhiked first by car, and then, in northern Canada, by bush airplane. Each plane dropped her off farther and farther north. Sometimes Laurie didn't see anybody for ten or twelve days, before the next plane came by. She says:

> It wasn't hard to entertain myself because it's so beautiful there, even up in the tundra. I'd just sit and watch the sky and the famous Canadian sunsets and the Northern Lights, which I had never seen before. Or I'd sit and watch my knife propped up against a rock reflecting the sunset and then reflecting the fire and then getting dark. There was always something to do. I love water, and I could always jump in the water.

Laurie got within two hundred miles of the North Magnetic Pole near Bathurst Island in northern Canada before turning back.

When she arrived in New York, she discovered that her beautiful loft had been brutally destroyed by vandals. Her books had been burned, her films torn up, the phones ripped out of the walls, and every window broken. Laurie recalls:

> I walked in from a trip where I had been trying to be very self-sufficient and I realized that now I really did have nothing, except this little knapsack that I had been traveling around with. That was an important time for me because while I missed having some of the things, I was thrilled with being out on my own in New York. Sometimes I stayed with friends, sometimes I just wandered around until I got another place. It was a very, very freeing time for me, because the trip itself had been one of the most wonderful experiences of my life.

Over the next five years, Laurie Anderson received a number of commissions to create works and perform them in Europe. She also composed several pieces for orchestra, including one commissioned by Dennis Russell Davies for the American Composers Orchestra. She based this piece, *It's Cold Outside*, on one of her earlier songs.

Anderson describes her pieces for orchestra as "forgettable." Something was missing in them. What makes Laurie Anderson's work *work* is Laurie Anderson performing it. Without her presence on the stage, without her words, without her electronic instruments, the music fell flat. She had already traveled on a road that was different from the one a traditional composer takes, and using a traditional medium like orchestra was not suitable for her material.

Early in her career, Laurie Anderson thought her work would always attract a small audience of people who were interested in the avant-garde; however, in 1978, she had an experience that changed her mind. The Museum of Contemporary Art in Houston sponsored a show of Laurie's work at the C & W Bar. Her performance was mistakenly billed as "some kind of country fiddling." The people who came to the C & W Bar expecting to hear bluegrass music got quite a surprise. After the show, some members of the audience came up to Laurie and said, "You know, it's weird, it's *weird!* But we liked it!"

Between 1979 and 1983, Anderson spent most of her time working on a huge seven-hour performance-art piece called *United States, Parts I–IV*. The work has been described as a "solo opera," "stylized lecture," "poetry reading with aural and visual imagery," "electric circus," "punk vaudeville"—in short, performance art.

Laurie composed "O Superman," probably her most famous song, to be included in *United States*. It is about an answering machine that takes the message that the world is about to end in nuclear destruction:

> *Hello? Is anybody home? Well, you don't know me,*
> *but I know you.*
> *And I've got a message to give to you.*
> *Here come the planes.*
> *So you better get ready. Ready to go. You can*
> *come as you are, but pay as you go.*

At the end of "O Superman," when impending doom is near, Anderson offers a phrase of consolation which turns into a warning to use modern technology with caution:

> *So hold me, Mom, in your long arms.*
> *In your automatic arms. Your petrochemical arms.*
> *Your military arms. In your electronic arms.*

Laurie speaks some of the lyrics of "O Superman" and sings others through an electronic instrument called a Vocoder. A Vocoder looks like an electronic keyboard or synthesizer but sounds like the player's voice. When Laurie speaks while pressing down a key on the Vocoder, it sounds as if she is singing the pitch she is playing. She presses down a whole chord, and it sounds as if she is singing in three-part harmony with herself.

"O Superman" is in the style of minimalist music. A strong pulse is set at the beginning of the song by a digital loop, a steady "ah-ah-ah" on a single note. The harmony through the song consists of only two chords, and the melody is constructed of only a few notes. The pulsing "ah-ah-ah" returns at the end of the song, then suddenly stops, without slowing down or fading away. The abrupt ending is another trait of minimalist music.

Laurie produced the recording of "O Superman" in her own studio, The Lobby, for about $400. She had a thousand copies of the record pressed, then sold them by mail order from her home. Business was slow at first, but then the song caught on in England. Laurie recalls, "All these people from England [called] saying, 'Can you ship about forty thousand, please?' I looked over at my little stack and said, 'Sure, I'll send them. You bet.' "

Obviously she needed a little help. She signed a recording contract with Warner Brothers Records, which mass-produced and distributed "O Superman." The song rose to number two on the pop charts in England, and grossed over a million dollars. All of this came as a big surprise to Laurie. "O Superman" may be the only hit single ever financed by a grant from the National Endowment of the Arts.

"O Superman" is only one of seventy-eight events that make up *United States*. Anderson groups these events—songs, musical and visual interludes, and little stories—into four parts, loosely based on the themes of transportation, politics, money, and love. Over the four-year period of her work, Anderson gave performances of the individual parts as she completed them. In 1983, Anderson put the whole thing together, presenting the seven-hour-long *United States: Parts I–IV* on two evenings at the Brooklyn Academy of Music.

Looming over the stage was a giant thirty-by-forty-foot screen on which Anderson projected 1,200 drawings, cartoons, photographs, and films. The stage itself was set with only a few prop tables and an assortment of microphones attached to a Vocoder. During the show, Anderson used the Vocoder to alter her voice from a high girlish soprano to a low, male voice of authority that has been described as "John Wayne selling used cars." Laurie says, "You find you have different things to say when you have a voice like that."

For the performance, Laurie Anderson wore all black—except for electric-pink socks—and a short, spiky hairstyle, which has become her trademark. She played her "tape-bow violin," equipped with a neon bar on the bow that glowed in the dark. Her prerecorded message was "Say what you mean and mean what you say."

For one segment of *United States*, Anderson wires her head with an amplifier and plays a drum solo on her own skull. The final boom of a brass drum resounds with a crunch of her teeth.

Anderson's electronic props represent the electronic clutter of the world. In her love song "Let X = X" stars don't come out at night; satellites do. She likes to look at one thing from two opposite viewpoints. For instance, the telephone can transmit highly impersonal communication or relate whispered secrets between friends.

In *United States* and in Anderson's other work, there is a lot of music and art going on all at once. "I try to make the experience as dense as possible," she says. However, the most important element of her work is her written material—her *words*. "I'm just a story-teller," she claims, "the oldest profession in the world." Her quirky stories possess a wry humor, but they are also vaguely disturbing, like waking up from a bad dream. For instance, in her low, male voice she says,

I came home today, and I opened the door with my bare hands. And I said, "Hey, who tore up all my wallpaper samples? Who ate all the grapes? The ones I was saving?" And this guy was sitting there, and I said, "Hey pal! What's going on here?" and he had this smile, and when he smiled he had these big white teeth like luxury hotels on the Florida coastline. And when he closed his mouth it looked like a big scar. And I said to myself, "Holy smokes—looks like some kind of guest-host relationship to me."

Warner Brothers released a five-record set called *United States Live* and a single-record album, *Big Science*, which includes some songs from the work. A companion book, *United States*, was published by Harper & Row. Some of the segments from the work are included on the home video *Laurie Anderson: Collected Videos*, released in 1989.

In 1986, Laurie Anderson created *Home of the Brave*, a feature film of her performance art. Here she mixes

Dressed as her cartoon character, Sharkey, Laurie Anderson explains the difference between zero and one in her video Home of the Brave
Courtesy of Laurie Anderson

some old material with some new ideas. In the opening number, "Good Evening," she dances with her violin hooked to a computer; she's dressed in a man's white suit, a skinny white tie, a black T-shirt, and a stocking mask that looks like her cartoon character, Sharkey. Other performers, also wearing stocking masks, walk around the stage like zombies, while on the big rear screen, drawings of planes, umbrellas, and TVs rain from the sky.

In *Home of the Brave*, Laurie performs in various languages, including Spanish, Japanese, and French.

Visual gags include a keyboard necktie that Laurie actually plays, a rubber-neck guitar that is used as a bat, a keyboard player dressed like a ballerina, who does barre exercises as she performs, floating shirts that the actors slip on, and a gigantic magnifying glass that Laurie holds before her face.

In "Zero and One," Anderson reasons:

Now nobody wants to be a zero. To be a zero means to be a nothing, a nobody, a has-been, a clod. On the other hand, almost everybody wants to be number one. To be number one means to be a winner, top of the heap, the acme, and there seems to be a strange national obsession with this particular number. Now, in my opinion, the problem with these numbers is that they're just too close, leaves very little room in there for everybody else, just not enough range. So first, we need to get rid of the value judgments attached to these two numbers and realize that to be a zero is no better, no worse than to be number one. Because . . . because what we are actually looking at here are the building blocks of the modern computer age.

The impact of *Home of the Brave* is marred somewhat by other filmmakers' wide range of special effects. When we watch Laurie play her drum suit, we are not convinced it's the real thing. We are more likely to suspect that she is merely slapping herself while a drummer in the background synchronizes his sound with her movement. This is a small criticism, however, and *Home of the Brave* gives many more people a chance to see Laurie Anderson in action. Excerpts from the music in *Home of the Brave* are included on her album *Mr. Heartbreak*, released in 1984.

In the summer of 1989, Laurie Anderson got out of a New York cab in front of her manager's office and dropped five and a half feet through an open manhole, an accident that drastically changed her outlook, much as Alice's tumble into a rabbit hole changed hers.

After being pulled out of the manhole, Laurie discovered that her knees were too injured to walk. An ambulance whisked her off to the hospital, where she waited her turn for medical attention in an overcrowded emergency room. An old homeless woman with swollen, bloody feet, wrapped in rags, said to Laurie, "Look at my feet, swollen up like grapefruit."

Laurie Anderson performs in Home of the Brave. *Photograph by Les Fincher*
Used by permission of Les Fincher, courtesy of Laurie Anderson

Laurie admits that she could not look; in fact, she turned her head the other way. However, a man sitting next to the woman slipped his arm around her shoulders and said, "Boy, that must really hurt."

The man's sympathetic response gave Laurie the idea for her song "Ramon," used in her ninety-minute performance-art piece *Empty Places* and in her recording *Strange Angels*.

Laurie Anderson performed *Empty Places* at the Brooklyn Academy of Music's 1989 Next Wave Festival. *Empty Places* has the usual high-tech electronic equipment and two thousand slides projected on four twenty-foot-high screens, but there's a big difference between *Empty Places* and Anderson's previous work. She says, "It's an unadorned story about pain and it doesn't have any imaginary items in it, like hosts of angels mowing our lawn. I wanted to have the whole of *Empty Places* feel more raw, more jagged than my past works."

The images Anderson choose for *Empty Places* are windblown branches, circling goldfish, and white birds gliding over water. Her irony is less playful and more biting. About equal pay for women, she states:

> You know, for every dollar a man makes a woman makes 63 cents. Now, 50 years ago that was 62 cents. So, with that kind of luck, it'll be the year 3888 before we make a buck.

Empty Places is more down-to-earth, steeped in hard, cold reality—and, for that reason, perhaps less interesting—than Anderson's previous work.

Another big difference in *Empty Places* and *Strange*

Angels is that Anderson took some singing lessons and put them to use. Gone are her spoken delivery, Vocoder techniques, and minimalist style. Her clear, high soprano and complex backup arrangements sound less avant-garde and more mainstream pop. Discovering her singing voice is very new to Laurie Anderson, but the result is a little old-hat for us.

Every artist has to try new things, and Laurie Anderson is still evolving. No doubt she has plenty more ideas stuffed in her bag of tricks. We just have to wait to see what comes up next.

SOME OTHERS

Grazyna Bacewicz (1913–69) Polish violinist who composed many violin works, including seven concertos. She learned to compose for orchestra while playing with the Symphony Orchestra of Polish Radio. She defied Hitler by remaining in Warsaw throughout World War II composing Polish music, including *Overture for Orchestra*, a dramatic musical reflection of the war.

Margaret Bonds (1913–72) Black American pianist and composition student of Florence Price who used material from African-American music in many of her works.

Lili Boulanger (1893–1918) Frenchwoman who, at age nineteen, won the Prix de Rome but had to enter this prestigious composition competition anonymously so that she would not be disqualified because she was a woman. She composed many fine choral works; however, her promising career was cut short when she died at the age of twenty-five. Lili's sister Nadia enjoyed a long life as an influential teacher of many composers, including Aaron Copland, Elliot Carter, and Philip Glass.

Cécile Chaminade (1857–1944) French pianist who composed over two hundred piano pieces, among other works, and was one of the first women to make a career of composing.

Pozzi Escot (1923–) Peruvian-born American professor who at age twenty-three was named Laureate Composer of Peru.

Elena Firsova (1950–) Member of a group of Russian composers who have broken away from government sponsorship to gain more artistic freedom in their works.

Varvara Andrianovna Gaigerova (1903–44) Russian pianist and concertmistress at the Bolshoi Theater who used material from the folk music of southeastern Russia in her compositions.

Miriam Gideon (1906–) American professor whose compositions include many chamber works for an unusual combination of instruments; *Rhymes from the Hill*, for example, uses voice, clarinet, cello, and marimba.

Peggy Glanville-Hicks (1912–) Australian who worked in the United States from 1942 to 1959. Her most famous work is the opera *The Transposed Heads* (1953); she has also composed orchestral, chamber, and vocal pieces.

Sofia Gubaidulina (1931–) A leading Russian composer who uses many avant-garde techniques.

Barbara Kolb (1939–) American clarinetist whose vigorous compositional style includes material from many sources.

Joan LaBarbara (1947–) American singer and writer who performs her own vocal compositions, has worked as a new-music critic and columnist for several newspapers, and often composes electronic music.

Josephine Lang (1815–80) German who studied composition with Felix Mendelssohn and published several books of songs, which were highly praised by critics and widely performed in her time.

Luise Adolpha LeBeau (1850–1927) German who was regarded in her time as the first important woman composer of opera and orchestral works.

Tania Leon (1944–) Black American pianist, conductor, and teacher who is the founder and music director of the Dance Theatre of Harlem Orchestra.

Elizabeth Maconchy (1907–) Englishwoman whose works, especially her fourteen string quartets, are influenced by Béla Bartók. Her operas, songs, and choral works sound more English.

Marianne von Martinez (1744–1812) Austrian pianist and singer who studied piano and composition with Joseph Haydn and performed piano duets with Wolfgang Mozart. She composed masses, vocal works, a symphony, two piano concertos, and two piano sonatas.

Mary Carr Moore (1873–1957) American conductor and singer who sang in her own operas and was the only woman to lead the eighty-man orchestra at the 1915 Panama-Pacific International Exposition when it performed her compositions.

Thea Musgrave (1928–) A native of Scotland who has composed five operas including *Mary, Queen of Scots* and *A Christmas Carol* among other works.

Pauline Oliveros (1932–) American conductor and professor who is outspoken about equal rights for women in music. Her numerous avant-garde works include many in the electronic medium.

Shulamit Ran (1949–) Israeli-born American pianist and professor who won the Pulitzer Prize for music in 1991.

Ruth Crawford Seeger (1901–53) American pianist who composed avant-garde works and transcribed over six hundred American folk songs. (See chapter five of *American Music Makers,* by Janet Nichols.)

Maria Szymanowska (1789–1831) Pianist and composer of ninety piano pieces who is considered the most important Polish composer before Chopin. Chopin knew Szymanowska, attended her concerts, and was greatly influenced by her work.

Germaine Tailleferre (1892–1983) A member of *Les Six,* a group of French composers who were influenced by Erik Satie and composed new styles of French music in reaction against nineteenth-century German Romantic music.

SUGGESTED LISTENING

LAURIE ANDERSON
Big Science
"O Superman"
Warner Brothers Records, 1982

Home of the Brave (video)
Warner Brothers, 1986

AMY BEACH
*Dark Garden: Songs, Violin Pieces,
and Piano Music*
Songs
"Ah, Love but a Day," Op. 44,
No. 2
"Just for This!" Op. 26, No. 2
Piano solo
"By the Still Waters," Op. 114
"A Humming-bird," Op. 128,
No. 3
Violin and piano
"Mazurka," Op. 40, No. 3
Northeastern

VIVIAN FINE
*Vivian Fine: Quartet for Brass,
Momenti, and Missa Brevis*
CRI (Composers Recordings, Inc.)

FANNY MENDELSSOHN
HENSEL
Klavierwerke, Vol. 2: Piano Music
"Il Saltarello Romano"
CPO Digital Recording, 1987

*Lili Boulanger, Fanny Hensel, Clara
Schumann: Choral Works and Songs*
"Gartenlieder" ("Garden
Songs")
Bayer Records, 1988

FLORENCE PRICE
*Althea Waites Performs the Piano
Music of Florence Price*
Dances in the Canebrakes
Cambria Records

CLARA SCHUMANN
Complete Works for the Piano, Vol. 1
Jozef De Beenhouwer, pianist
Soirées Musicales, Op. 6
Partridge

*Lili Boulanger, Fanny Hensel, Clara
Schumann: Choral Works and Songs*
*Drei gemischte Chore (Three
Choral Works) (1848)*
Bayer Records

ETHEL SMYTH
*The Plymouth Music Series: Mass
in D*
"Kyrie" (from Mass in D)
"March of the Women"
Virgin Classics Limited

BARBARA STROZZI
*Glenda Simpson Sings Barbara
Strozzi with The Camerata of
London*
"Gite, o giorni dolenti" ("Pass,
O Sorrowful Days")
"Amore e bandito" ("Love Is
Banished!")
Hyperion Records Limited

JOAN TOWER
*Meet the Composer Orchestra
Residency Series: Joan Tower*
Leonard Slatkin conducts the St.
Louis Symphony Orchestra
Sequoia
Elektra/Nonesuch Records

Joan Tower: Amazon, Wings, Noon
Dance, Platinum Spirals
   Wings
CRI (Composers Recordings, Inc.)

ELLEN TAFFE ZWILICH
Chamber Symphony, String Quartet,
Sonata in Three Movements
   Chamber Symphony
CRI (Composers Recordings, Inc.)

FOR FURTHER READING

American Music Makers, by Janet Nichols (Walker and Co., 1990)

Clara Schumann: The Artist and the Woman, by Nancy B. Reich (Cornell University Press, 1985)

Contributions of Women: Music, by Catherine Scheader (Dillon Press, 1985)

Felix Mendelssohn: His Life, His Family, His Music, by Herbert Kupferberg (Charles Scribner & Sons, 1972)

United States, by Laurie Anderson (Harper & Row, 1982)

Women Making Music, edited by Jane Bowers and Judith Tick (University of Illinois Press, 1987)

GLOSSARY

accompaniment the part of the music that supports the main melody or soloist

alto low female voice

aria lyrical piece for solo voice, often with orchestral accompaniment, which is sometimes part of an opera

art song piece of vocal music that is written in the tradition of classical music, unlike folk, jazz, and pop songs

avant-garde artists and musicians who experiment with new art forms, which are not usually understood or accepted by the general public

Baroque adjective used to describe music written between 1600 and 1750

bass low male voice

cantata lengthy vocal work, with instrumental accompaniment, that is often divided into sections for soloists, small groups of voices, and chorus

chamber music compositions for one or a few musicians, which can be played in a small room rather than a large concert hall

chord combination of three or more notes sounded together

choreography a set of steps and other movements for dancers

classical adjective used to describe music written between 1750 and 1825

commission formal request to a composer to write a specific type of composition, often for a specific occasion; usually presented with a gift of money to help support the composer while she writes the piece

concerto large composition for orchestra and solo instrument, usually divided into three movements

conservatory music school

consonance combined tones that create a feeling of rest; the opposite of dissonance

contemporary   adjective used to describe music written after 1900; also, "twentieth-century."

counterpoint   two or more melodies played at once

dissonance   combined tones that clash, creating restlessness; the opposite of consonance

duet   piece written for two performers

duple meter   two beats per measure

ensemble   group of musicians

folk music   music that consists mostly of songs, created by people who have no musical training, and passed down from generation to generation without being written down.

harmony   chords that support a melody; also, the study of how chords are formed and how they follow each other

improvise   create music while performing it

jazz   a style of music with syncopated rhythms that is usually improvised; developed in the United States, predominantly by black musicians, in the first half of the twentieth century

key   the most important note, chord, and scale of a composition.

leitmotif   recurring musical theme in an opera, which represents a person, object, or idea

librettist   person who writes the text of an opera

libretto   text of an opera

lied   German word for "song." The plural is *lieder*.

lyrics   words of a song

madrigal   vocal work usually set for a small, unaccompanied ensemble of singers

Mass   church service in the Catholic and some Protestant religions; frequently set to music and often performed in a concert setting

measure   rhythmic group containing a certain number of beats marked off on a score by vertical lines

meter   a group of beats, in which the first one is strongest

minimalist music   a style of music with a strong beat, many repetitions of short melodies, and few changes in dynamics and harmony; developed in the 1960s

motive a short musical idea that is developed throughout a composition

movement part of a large composition that has its own melodic, rhythmic, and harmonic structure

multi-movement describes a composition that has more than one movement; usually performed with pauses between the movements

musicologist person who studies music and music history

nationalism a style of nineteenth-century music in which a composer uses folk songs, dances, legends, and other national material of his or her homeland

notate write down a musical idea

opus (Abbreviation: op.) Latin word for "work." A number that tells in what order a composer's work was published

orchestration arranging a composition for orchestra; choosing which instruments will play each part of the music

patron wealthy person who donates money toward the support of a composer or the cost of producing his or her music

performance art work of art that is not complete until the artist sets it into motion by playing music, singing, reciting, acting, and dancing, or through some electronic means

piece composition that is played on musical instruments

quartet ensemble of four performers; also, a piece written for four performers

quintet ensemble of five performers; also, a piece written for five performers

ragtime a style of jazz developed in the 1890s, usually for solo piano, usually in duple meter, with a marchlike tempo

register part of the total range of a musical instrument or voice; for example, a register could be described as low, mid-range, or high

Romantic adjective used to describe music written between 1825 and 1900

salon room in a palace or private home that is known for the concerts performed there

scale   the notes of a key, ordered from the lowest to the highest

score   written version of a musical composition

sonata   composition for solo instrument, which often includes a piano accompaniment

song   composition that is sung

soprano   high female voice

string quartet   ensemble that includes two violins, one viola, and one cello; also, a composition written for string quartet

suite   set of short pieces having related subject matter

symphony   composition written for orchestra; also, an orchestra

syncopation   accenting a note at an unexpected time, as on a weak beat or between two beats

tempo   speed at which a composition is played

tenor   high male voice

theme   melody that is used several times within a movement or composition

theory   the study of the structure of music, including rhythm, melody, harmony, form, ear training, style, counterpoint, and orchestration

timbre   quality of sound that makes one instrument or voice sound different from another; also called tone color

trio   ensemble of three performers; also, a piece written for three performers

triple meter   three beats per measure

vibrato   small fluctuation of pitch of a single note in performance by singers and string and wind instrument players

virtuoso   highly skilled musician

Vocoder   electronic instrument that allows a performer to sing any pitch she selects by simultaneously pressing down a key on a keyboard

word painting   in songs, music that represents an image in the lyrics; for example, fast notes sung on the word "running," or one person singing on the word "alone"

INDEX

Accademia degli Unisoni, 6–7
African-American music, 114, 118, 119, 120, 125, 203
Alexander, Kathryn, 164
All-women orchestras, 99, 103–4
American Academy and Institute of Arts and Letters, 142
American Composers Alliance (ACA), 138
American Composers Orchestra, 143, 160, 193
American Conservatory of Music, 117, 129
American musicians
    prejudice against, 93–94, 104, 169
American Society of Composers, Authors, and Publishers (ASCAP), 124, 138
American Symphony Orchestra, xiv, 124, 173, 179
Anderson, Laurie, xiv, 182*f*, 198*f*, 200*f*, 209
    works, 186–87, 188–89, 193–96, 197–200, 201–2
Anderson, Marian, 116–17
Arkansas Music Teachers Association, 117
Art music/songs, 116, 137–38
Avant garde, 129, 193, 202, 204, 206

Babbitt, Milton, 136
Bacewica, Grazyna, 203

Bach, Johann Sebastian, 2, 17, 95
Baermann, Carl, 95
Barbirolli, Sir John, 123–24
Bard College, 160, 166
Barnby, Sir Joseph, xiv, 74
Baroque era, 1, 11, 130
Barthé, Richmond, 119
Bartholdy, Jakob, 18, 20, 24
Bartók, Béla, 108, 205
Beach, Amy (Mrs. H. H. A. Beach), xiii, 92*f*, 93–109, 125, 209
    place in musical history, 108–9
    works, 95, 99–100, 101, 102, 105–107, 108
Beach, Henry Harris Aubrey, 96–98, 101
Beecham, Sir Thomas, 80, 87, 104–5
Beethoven, Ludwig van, 62, 68, 73, 86–87, 95, 98, 154, 155
Belleville, Anna Caroline de, 43
Bennington College, 139, 154, 156
Berger, Arthur, 132
Berger, Ludwig, 17
Berlin Philharmonic, 101
Berlioz, Hector, 68, 96
Bigot, Marie, 17
Black spirituals, 116–17, 120
Blacks, xii, 111–25, 203
Blahetica, Leopoldine, 43
Bonds, Estella C., 119